The Final Hours

The Final Hours

*Farewell letters from the executed
Danish patriots*

Translated from the Danish by Brian Young

Preface by

Bishop H. Øllgaard

Copenhagen

BERLINGSKE FORLAG
1946

*Boys, you boys who died,
you lit in Denmark's deepest gloom
a shining sunrise.*
Kaj Munk

New Nordic Press 2017

ISBN 9780989601023
LCCN 2017909090
New Nordic Press
Port Townsend, WA
www.newnordicpress.com
Cover painting by Else Young
Cover layout by Marita Sempio
Printed by Lightning Source
Printed in the United States of America

A note from the translator and editor

"The Final Hours" was first published in Denmark in 1946. This is the first English translation of this collection of letters.

It is difficult to give an exact figure for the number of Danes who were killed (in Denmark) during the five years of the German occupation. Hans Kirchhoff sets that number at 2685. According to official records, 112 members of the resistance were arrested and executed by German court martial between August 28, 1943 and April 25, 1945. It is those resistance members, sentenced to death, who were allowed to write farewell letters on the eve of their execution. This book contains all 78 of those letters.

This collection of letters was first published in 1946. Originally, my plan was to translate a "selection" of these letters, which span a wide range of writing talent, from simple and very short, to long and very poetic and impassioned. But I came to the conclusion that I could not pick and choose between them. That was something that I felt I had no right to do. So it was all of them.

I offer no comments or evaluation. The letters speak for themselves. I will only point out the following:

The alphabetical register in the back of the original book contains 114 names. Eight of those are not otherwise mentioned in the book. They were active in the resistance, but their fates are not mentioned here.

There are 28 names of members of the resistance who appear with photos and short bios, but did not have letters included in the collection.

That leaves 78 members of the resistance who were executed by the Nazis. Their letters, their last letters, are given here.

(The translated Danish text begins on page VII, and ends on page 132. The appendix was not part of the original text)

Preface

During the German occupation of Denmark, according to official declarations, 112 Danish freedom fighters were tried and executed by the German court martial.

The first execution was carried out as late as August 28, 1943, which was a turning point in the history of the occupation, when the Danish people said No to the German demands. After that the number of executions increased, while at the same time incidents of sabotage grew, as did the acts of German reprisal. Six executions took place in the last 5 months of 1943, while during the period from March 1945 until April 25, no fewer than 62 executions were carried out.

Most of these men were young; the average age wasn't much more than 25 years, and they had all been active in the Danish resistance.

We will never forget the impression it made on us when we received the news of their deaths. I remember a young man who paced back and forth in my room, pale and saddened, yet at the same time even more eager to join up, and move deeper into the struggle. The resentment against the Germans grew, and the decision to fight against them was strengthened and confirmed. The risk of being caught and tortured no longer scared us. There is no doubt, that for each one who fell, 10, 20, or even more volunteered for the dangerous work.

After being sentenced to death, these young men were usually given permission to write, during the last few hours they to had live, one last farewell letter to their closest family. These letters helped to console not only those they were sent to, but others often read them as well, as people were so close to each other in those days. Many letters were copied and shared, and reprinted in the underground newspapers. Even people who didn't know those who were executed felt comfort and encouragement, and this helped to solidify the resistance *movement. In this way, the dead, through their letters, were still in the fight, and inspired those who were left behind.*

Now we have collected together many of these farewell letters, so that they may speak with clarity to our time, and the times to come, of the courage and devotion in the fight for Denmark's freedom. They were all written without any thought of publication; and though they are not all literary works of art, they are all human documents of the highest class.

There might be some uniformity in these letters, as they were all written in the same circumstances—with the certainty of death looming. But this uniformity establishes certain things that are very important. First of all we must admire the resolve and calm with which they accepted their fate. One of them writes "that I have to die now is not something I can be happy about, it wouldn't be natural at my age; but the way it will happen is quite alright." They are often surprised at how easily they face their situation, but they realize that this is because they do not regret that they joined the fight, even though it cost them their life. They realized the truth in the verse— "always confident", which is so often repeated:

Fight for all you care for, die if that's what's needed, then life is not that hard, and death will not be either.

And many of them knew for sure that God would not forsake them. One, who in his farewell letter to his parents signed it with "Your happy son," had just before said: "As long as you believe in God, then you have nothing to fear."

This thing about God is something they had probably not talked about before, but being face to face with death, the inhibitions that had bound them fell away, and in the letters they open up and express their deepest feelings. "I'm not used to saying what I feel," but now they had to try. That which was most important to say was the son's gratitude to his family, and the man's to his own home. "It's first now that I realize how much loving parents mean in life; if you have them then you can face anything." And then comes a prayer for forgiveness, because they had not always behaved as they should have. They wanted to spare their loved ones. There is no hint of the torture that most of them had been subjected to.

If there are parents who are having problems with their grown children, then they should read these letters, and learn how there are the strongest bonds, even if the young do not express it in their daily life.

Yes, read these letters, and learn from them to believe in Denmark's youth!

Read these letters and realize how they oblige us to fight for their ideals, so the one who writes: "No matter what, it meant something," can be right!

Read these letters with respect for these young freedom fighter's sacrifices.

As in a game they joined in the bloody dance, and died for Denmark's honor. *

Odense Bishops Palace, September 1945.

* From an inscription on a monument in the Odense Cemetery over the Danish soldiers who fell in 1848-50

The First Execution

Designer Paul Edvin Kjær Sørensen, who was executed by the Germans on 28 August 1943, was the first to die. His application for a pardon, which went through the Danish foreign ministry, was denied. Based on a conversation that the public prosecutor had with the German chaplain, we can give some information on the first *execution, and on Paul Sørensen's final hours*

Paul heard from a German officer in the morning of 28 August, at 2:30 a.m., that his pardon had been denied, and that the execution would soon take place. Soon afterwards a German chaplain showed up in his cell, and stayed with Paul for about one hour. The chaplain said that Paul was completely at ease during the conversation, and that he was given the cigarettes that he wanted. They talked about Paul's father, his siblings, and girlfriend, and also about his deceased mother, who he would soon be reunited with.

About 4:45 a.m. a car showed up, and Paul, accompanied by the chaplain and two German soldiers, was driven outside of the town. When they arrived at the place, Paul was led into an open courtyard, and the officer on watch read the sentence of execution one more time, and asked him if he had any wishes. Paul said that he would prefer not to be blindfolded, and that he wanted another cigarette. These wishes were granted. Then Paul said to the chaplain that he had such a good pullover, and that he wanted to take it off so that his brother could get it. This wish was also granted. The chaplain stepped to one side, and the execution was carried out. A German doctor observed it, and declared that death was instantaneous. According to the chaplain's account to the public prosecutor, Paul was completely at ease to the very end.

In order to avoid unrest in connection with the burial of the first Dane to be executed, the Germans took the body to Warnemunde, where, according to German information, it was interned. At the same time, two letters were sent to his father, foreman Oluf Sørensen, through the police chief in Aarhus. One of those letters is printed here.

List of those executed who wrote final letters

Paul Edvin Kjær Sørensen

28 August 1943 (6 June 1916)

Dear Dad

I have been sent to Copenhagen, and when you read this letter, I will no longer be.

The application for a pardon has been rejected; so now I have to, in this way, say goodbye to all of you, now don't take this too hard, but forgive me, for having caused you such great sorrow.

I would like to lie alongside my mother, if that can be arranged.

Goodbye, dear Father, Sister and Brother, say hello to all of my family.

Your devoted, Paul

PS. If there is anything that Else wants of my things, then give it to her.

(Share with her, Dad)

Svend Eduard Rasmussen

22 November 1943 (30 December 1905)

My beloved Gutte!

This is the last greeting that I can send to you, for this morning I shall die. I am so sorry that I cannot, before that, see you and my dear Finn. There is so much that I want to say to you, little Gutte, but it is as if that cloud that will soon descend upon me, is making me blind and mute. But you must at least know, that I love you and Finn with a love that I have been way too shy to express in everyday life. If I have been a good husband and father, I don't know? there is so much that happens when we live without the thought of death. But you know that I am not a bad person, and that I have only acted according to those impulses that, for me, have been the right ones.

And now I will have to pay for that with my life.

Finally, I ask you, beloved friend, console yourself soon, you must not give up for life's harshness, imagine that I could have died from natural causes, then it would not be so hard. I don't believe that there is a life after this one, all the unlikely and horrible things, that happen in this world, I don't think they are a sign of an all-wise Power, but if there is a continuation, then I will watch over you two, who are my only things in the world, and that still give me such terrible pain to have to leave in that way.

Now goodbye to both of you, and be sweet to greet Ejner and his sister, I have also thought about them. If only I could kiss you goodbye.

Live well.

Your Svend

Marius Peder Kristian Jeppesen

22 November 1943 (21 April 1922)

Beloved Mom!

My sentence today is death, but you must be good, because I will be meeting Dad and Granddad Hans Peter up there with Jesus. I will also be meeting you, dear Mom.

Your son Marius

A pastor was here with me today; I went to communion, dear Mom. I will meet you in heaven, so be well here on the Earth. Greet all my dear brothers, my beloved sister, family and friends from your beloved son, who is now going to heaven to dear Jesus. Be well, I'm not crying, I am going peacefully to die. The pastor will be here when I go to heaven.

Marius Jeppesen

Dear Mom!

George Goritz Mørk Christiansen

29 November 1943 (14 September 1921)

Dear Mom.

I have not yet heard anything about my application for a pardon, so I find myself, quite honestly, in a rather tense state of mind. I am after all a philosopher, and, though not a great one, at least one of those who takes life's ups and downs, including its end, with minimal agitation, as I cannot stop looking at everything with a certain amount of skepticism. When I anyhow feel rather depressed, then it is mostly for your sake, because I cannot, despite your lovely and honorable assurances to the contrary, avoid feeling that I have failed you and your dreams. When I think back through the years on everything that you have been for me, how patient and devoted, and how much you cared for your two children, then I feel so weak, and get tears in my eyes, which I normally consider a symptom to be avoided.

In general I don't believe it's the best medicine against a situation like my present one, to be looking back on all the joy and happiness that you have experienced in this life, but on the other hand it can be a good trump card to have, when the doubts come with their cold shadows and ask: "What did you really get out of it all?" Yes, I know it is said, that when you are in your seventies, you have reached your full maturity, but you must remember, that always later, when you look back, you see childhood and youth as the real life. It is in those years that you take in the whole world. I believe that, for most, it has already been decided, before the twenty years have gone, if the individual will be a wimp, or a man who can weather life's hardest storms. For that reason, already by that time, you have gotten an understanding of human life, and what life really is.

2 December. Dear Mom. Today I had to suddenly get up in the middle of the night. I am afraid this means the end. My lawyer had though said that I could count on a pardon. Goodbye Mom, and thanks for your kindness. Goodbye Grethe, and little Jens, who I had never seen.

Live well, George

Sven Chr. Johannesen

2 December 1943 (10 June 1923)

(After Sven had been told the time of his execution, he was allowed to write a farewell letter to his parents. However, they never received it. In the letter he gave an account of why he had to act the way he had, and the Germans found it to be so convincing that they feared it would be like a bright torch that would inspire other young people to follow his example. For that reason the letter was never sent to his parents, but was included with the case documents. Only through a concerted effort by Director Kjær of the Red Cross, in Aarhus, was the Director in Copenhagen allowed to read the letter, and copy the ending for his parents.)

Dear poor Dad and Mom

Now I will say to you, Dad and Mom, so many thanks for all that you have done for me. I know that I have often hurt you, and I ask your forgiveness for that. I didn't do it out of malice, but only from thoughtlessness, spite, and egoism. It has been a beautiful, beautiful childhood that I have had. I know that you have done your utmost so that I could have it good, and make my way in the world. I want to say many thanks for that.

Well, previously I had not thought much about God's presence, but now I believe, that I know, that there is one who controls everything, and when I die, then it is God's will. I have just received three letters from you. Dad writes, that in your opinion God forbids it. The ways of God are not for us to comprehend, and I am now certain that it is God's will, so I am at peace. I can die in peace. I have just been to communion. God's will be done.

(Even though Sven's parents only received a partial copy of his last letter, they anyhow received a written greeting from him after his death, as he had written, on the back of a stamp that he had with him in the prison, the King's motto:

"My God, my Country, my Honor"

Oluf Axelbo Kroer

2 December 1943 (17 April 1916)

Dear Mom and dear everyone!

Well, now it's over, but there was so much that I wanted to say to all of you. My hands are shaking a little, not because I am afraid, but because I know that the coming time will be worse for you than for me.

Yes, dear Mom, thanks for everything that you have been for me, you, who had to be both Dad and Mom for all of us, you have always been the ideal of a Mom for me. And dear Edith, Erik and Borge, thanks to you too. We have after all lived together in a way that is rare for siblings. I know that it is not necessary to ask you to take care of Mom, who has already had to bear a great sorrow. I have just received your letters, and have sat and read through them, and they have given me strength. Ida and Knud have also written, and especially Ida's little letter has made me happy. Say hello to them, and say thanks. Also say hello to them in the bank, and give them my thanks for the good collegiality. I have just spoken with a German pastor, and Mom, you should know, that I will meet death as a believer, that I know that we will meet again, so it isn't all that hard. I am thinking about that little verse:

Fight for all that you hold dear,

It's first now that I grasp the full meaning.

Dear Mom, I know of course, that you will read this letter many times, and if only I could write so that it would give you some solace. Now I will go to communion with my comrades, may they be just as much at peace as I am now. And now goodbye

God be with all of you Your Oluf

Anders Wilhelm Andersen

2 December 1943 (12 July 1924)

Dear Dad and Mother — everyone.

Well—now it's over. I just found out that I was not pardoned. I only have two hours to live. When you get this letter, I will be dead. Now you must not lose hope, but try to get over it.—I know full well that it's hard for you to lose two sons in one year—but it is God's will, and His ways are mysterious. I hope that you will always have fond memories of me — even though I have not always acted as I should have. Now you must try to arrange things so that you can live a quiet and peaceful life, and take care of Erik, Preben, Inga, Ellen, and Berth—yes, what does Bertha say? I would have liked to talk with her; she was after all that one of my sibling that I was fondest of. Give my greetings to Hans, and Mr. and Mrs. Møller, tell them thanks for the time we knew each other. They are great people, and God will watch over them. With respect to my boss—Rasmussen—say hello to him and his wife from me, and say that I hope that his faith in young people has not been broken—I didn't do it myself—I mean—it was, like it wasn't myself—I had to get out —
— —

My dearest Dad and Mother, it's first now that I know what loving parents mean in life, when you have them, then you can take everything in stride—I know, that they understand one.

Mom—Dad, I am going proudly and peacefully into eternity, as I know, that as long as you believe in God, then you have nothing to fear. Dad and Mom, may God bless you.

The last loving greetings from your happy son.

Anders.

Otto Manley Christiansen

2 December 1943 (30 September 1924

Dear Dad and Mom

First I want to say many thanks for all the good things you have done for me while I have been in prison here in Aarhus. And then I want to say many thanks for all the good things you have done for me in my whole life. I have just this morning received the message that I am to die, so now I'm sitting here, writing a farewell letter to you.

My greatest wish is that you can be at peace, because I am at peace, I have put my entire life in God's hands, and can only do what is right, so I am quite at ease. Mom, you must not lose courage, I am only being punished because I have sinned against God. If you knew how much I loved you and all of my siblings, but I never thought about that before, so now I have to say it to you. Mom, you shall have my watch, and you must wear it every day, so that way you will feel that I am close. Dad, you shall have all my clothes, as a little thanks for all the good things you have done for me. And I am also asking you to send one of my things to each of my siblings, and ask them to keep them in memory of me. No matter what, don't lose heart, but be happy that I can die in the belief that God is taking me home to him.

And finally, give my greetings to all of my friends and acquaintances.

With love

Otto

Alf Tolboe Jensen

29 December 1943 (14 September 1918)

Dear Dad and Mom!

You can believe that one gets time to think about many things during this time, things that you had almost never thought about before, and you start to look differently at things, that you had previously taken for granted.

I'm not sitting here alone, which I am very thankful for, it's always a relief and comfort to have an understanding person, and a good comrade, to talk with.

I don't understand why you are proud of my behavior, because I am not any different than I could be with my belief in God, and I agree completely when you write, that the only thing that can help is the faith you grew up with. I know that now, and I am convinced of it.

With loving regard and thoughts

Your son Alf

(And two hours before his execution, at 8:32 a.m., 29 December 1943)

Dear Dad and Mom

Well, now it's happened, I had counted on a pardon, as so much time has passed, but that hope was in vain.

Please give my greetings to everyone in Brabrand, and to you I send my best wishes, and ask for forgiveness for the wrong I have done you, as I have regrettably not always acted as you might have wished. And now at last my loving regards to you

Your son

Greetings to Grandpa and Grandma

Niels Stenderup

24 April 1944 (20 May 1924)

Dear everyone—

Five minutes ago I got the final answer; no pardon; in 1 1/2 hours it will happen. If it can be of any comfort to you, I am really not afraid. Of course I would have wanted to live longer, but at some time we will all be going this way. As for you, then I would prefer that you try to forget about me as quickly as possible; that is the principle that I have lived by. It doesn't help to carry a departed with you all through life; but it's probably hopeless to give any advice about that, I guess you can only act according to your own conscience, but you can take it as a wish, which for Inger's sake I can at least hope for; after all she has her whole life ahead of her.

I'm sorry that I'm not any better at expressing thanks for the years that have gone by, but I hope that I have, despite everything, shown some gratitude. Maybe I am more grateful for everything now than ever before, because I feel in a way that it is easier to die when you have really gotten something out of life. Thanks for that, both Dad and Mom and my aunt and everyone.

Mom said that grandma thought that all of this could have been avoided if she and auntie had not been in Copenhagen that day; that is as wrong as it can be. If it hadn't happened that day, then it would have happened on another. Anyone who knows a little about my psychology could confirm that!

There is not much more to say. Please give my greetings to everyone I knew.

Farewell, and try, like I said, to forget.

Niels

Svend Otto Nielsen

27 April 1944 (29 August 1908)

Dearest Mom.

You have probably already found out that I am no longer among the living. Don't cry over me, dear Mom, we all have to die, so get over it, dear Mom, as soon as possible. I am taking this quite easily, not at all afraid, I hope that I am going over to a better world. You have been a good mother to me. More loving people than you can't be found. I have suffered from a guilty conscience these last 5 months—that I have not been more for you.

Thanks for the happy moments we have had together. I have relived my life all over again during these lonesome 5 months, and so many times in that connection you have been in my thoughts. You have many times led me with a gentle hand in my childhood years; no one has had a better mother than me.

I hope that you live for many happy years yet, let your love for me go to benefit my little daughter.

My last affectionate greetings   Svend

Cell Nr. 65. 3 a.m. April 27, 1944

Dear brother, sister-in-law, and little Poul!

You probably wonder why I am writing in ink, which is not the normal thing; but this is also a very unusual time. Yesterday I had my beautiful full beard shaved off, and I figured that must have been a sign of something, and sure enough, today I was driven to Dagmar house.

The court marshal was scheduled for 1:20 P.M., I was sentenced to death, and taken back to my cell. At 2:30 P.M. the judge came and said that the sentence had been confirmed, and would be carried out at 6 A.M., so I have three hours left to live.

Until now I have taken this with unusual ease, almost with a hint of a smile, and if God is willing, I will meet death in the same way. I want to die with honor.

Dear friends, I am sending you one last thank you for what you have been for me, and I wish with all my heart that you may live well together. You have hopefully many years left to live in, use them well to forgive each other. You never know when God will be calling you, and then it is too late to make good that which you have neglected.

Now it's over, I wonder if I'll hear the shot, or die before?

Well, we'll soon see. I am not afraid to die, and I hope I don't become afraid, but I shouldn't boast too early, there might be limits to courage.

It has been beautiful weather today. I enjoyed the drive to Dagmar house. I thought it might be my last. It has been a real Danish spring day, I think, it bodes well for our beloved land; that is my wish, may good old Denmark experience free days again, may our countrymen delight and rejoice over all the beauty that surrounds us here.

I am sending a letter to mom, and a letter for Grethe I'll send to you, as I don't know her address; furthermore I am sending a little greeting to my colleagues, who have been so faithful to me during these five difficult months.

Please give my letter to Grethe as soon as possible. Tell her, that my last thoughts are about her and old Denmark. I wish so much that she may experience happiness, if she can just find a man who can be something for her and my little daughter. Take care of them. Be something for my little girl. She is my flesh and blood, remember that.

Excuse my disconnected thoughts, but I am so tired, I haven't been up so many hours in many months, and I am not healthy yet either.

I would have been an invalid anyhow, so I am not missing out on much by dying.

Now I have two hours left to live, and will finish.

With loving greetings to all of you, and the best wishes

May God be with you

With loving greetings   Svend

4:45 a.m., Thursday, April 27, 1944

Beloved Grethe girl, and little Kirsten!

In a couple of hours I will be no more. God's will be done!

I realize now what our little daughter has meant for us, oh, how I wish I could take her in my arms and press a father's kiss on her cheek, the little charmer, now you will have to do it for me.

Grethe girl, don't grieve over me, I don't want that, be sensible, you can't change anything in what has happened. Even I am cold and calm, I accepted my sentence without complaint or nervousness, with a little smile on my lips, yes, that's how you become, and these five months have hardened me. You know, my life has been rich in experience, unusually eventful in consideration of the few years I have lived. These last months have not been any less rich in experience. I have had plenty of time to think about life. I would have wanted to be out in life again and continue it together with you and our little girl to make up for my offenses, but God's will be done, He knows what is best for us.

I've had a vision several times: You standing under a light green hardwood tree with little Kirsten girl at your side. You stood with outstretched   arms, and greeted dad, who you hadn't seen in a long time, I thought maybe I would get out again, but we'll meet again for sure, Grethe, I believe in a life after death, do you also believe that, my girl, let's see each other again. Teach our little girl, that there is something that guides the world and gives peace in our souls.

It is now five A.M., I have just had some nice pieces of bread, and I am enjoying coffee with a good old-fashioned cigar. Remember now, the tradition from our "little, light, happy home". Only I can't jump around like I could then, I have lost the use of my limbs, but you know that.

May the Almighty now let me go peacefully to my death, as He has given me the strength to bear these painful months.

I wish for peace in the world, soon, peace in your mind, peace and happiness for our little land, and in my last prayer, I will pray for your future. The most loving thoughts and greetings

Svend

Lars Bager Svane

29 April 1944 (26 April 1919)

Beloved Mom!

They came! — It's 3 A.M., I have two hours left to live in. I am so young, so I thought that there was so much for me to live for, but I am not afraid to die; I knew the risks when I started on this work. Denmark will soon forget me, but I don't regret what I have done for my beloved country. Many will follow after me, but one beautiful day Denmark will be free again, so it will not have been in vain. The Guards might die, but it will never perish.

Dear Mom, everyday you read, with the greatest peace of mind, about the thousands that are killed— try to take my death with the same peace of mind, I am just one of the many. Greet Dad from me, he'll soon come home, you'll see, and you will have many good years left together. Thanks for my beautiful childhood, and everything since. Promise me Mom, don't grieve over me, I am not worth that. I have the chaplain with me, and that makes me feel safe and quiet. I would like to be buried by a church, and sing "Everything is Cheerful when you go", especially the last verse I have tried to live by. I thought there was so much I wanted to say to you, Mom, but now it seems like my brain is empty, I guess that is understandable. Thanks for all the goodness you have shown me in the time I was here.

Live well, all my beloved

Your Lars

George Brockhoff Quistgaard

20 May 1944 (19 February 1915)

Beloved Mom!

So comes the worst. Well, not for me, it won't be hard for me, but for you. But you have been unbelievable, and you will continue to be so. You will need all of your courage, but so far you have never failed. And then I know that you will be convinced that, despite everything, that it mattered! That isn't much comfort to give you, but when you know, that it's enough for me, then it will also mean something for you.

Why you now, again, have to lose someone, I don't understand. But try to think about not just what you lose, but what we have had. I know what Dad meant, and still means, for you, and in the same way we two will also always be together. And you have already given me so much good, that I am not able to be bitter, that there won't be any more. There was so much, that I could regret, and so much that I could and should have done, that I never did. But I won't use the time to regret, I will just be so deeply happy to think about how well we understood each other, even when I went my own strange ways.

It will be an extremely hard time for you, at first. But you mustn't forget, for a minute, how much you still have. Not just Bodil, but Bodil's boys. They are a fresh beginning, and you can teach them so much of that, which you had taught me. Why it always has to be you who gives, I don't know, but it must be good to be able to give something.

I'm probably not expressing myself very well tonight, I'm not used to saying what I feel, and it has not been necessary between us. We cared for each other, and will continue to care for each other, just that simple and everlasting.

And be convinced of this, and let it help you if it can, that this is strangely easy for me. It has not been in vain, and for that reason it is quite simple.

Be happy and well, dearest Mom.

Your son loves you., George

Arne Lutzen Hansen

24 May 1944 (19 February 1915)

Dear everyone

Today Søren is 7 months. I was so happy to see him yesterday. And even though it's German guns that have shot me, he must not be raised to hate it. He must learn that the most important thing in life is love, and after that tolerance, and then tolerance, and then tolerance again.

The last book I read, "Jørgen Stein", was also the best I have read yet. It seemed to echo so many of my opinions. Jacob Paludan must have been a man cast in the right mold. Søren must learn the negativity of the word "revenge". Forgiveness is the only right thing. You can be speechless when you see the delusion of the masses, and feel like just giving it all up with a shrug of the shoulders. But you must not do that; if we are to have it better here on earth, then you have to begin with yourself.

Lissen, just call him Arne anyway.

Promise me, everyone, to act according to what I wrote in my last letters.

When Søren is to be a soldier, ask him to read "Under the Eternal Stars", and "Jørgen Stein."

It's strange, I am already sitting here, and am a bit curious about what's behind all this earthly life. I have not really become convinced. I am most sorry thinking about how you will take it. I wonder if you have already heard, I hope not. Hopefully you will first hear later in the day. The time is now 1:00 a.m.

It's really not as bad as I thought. I hope you get this, my last letter.

During the days that have gone by since my sentencing, I have not been able to keep from smiling, at times, at all this theater. It was, after all, not a farce.

Call interpreter Ericksen at the prison, when you have calmed down, and greet him from me.

Maybe life would have become a hell for me, who knows, I saw life from a higher perspective, and in many ways had trouble approving of it. There was so much in the world that I could not accept. Now I am free of those troubles.

Don't forget to read my last two letters, I am not writing this so that you should wallow in the memory of me, but just so that you won't forget my last wishes.

I'm thinking a lot about Mom right now. Pull yourselves together. It is, after all, not so bad. Hopefully you have not already gotten the message.

Remember now: charity and tolerance.

Now none of you should do anything stupid in the first horrible hours. Not too many sleeping pills. That would make me feel sorry, and I might be sitting some place on a cloud watching you.

I was so fond of all of you. And that is not something I just now realize. And you know that well.

Just now I am wondering how Lissen will manage. Dad and Mom, you must help her, if you can. Not just now, but also in the future. You can let Søren be a substitute for me.

It's a comfort for me to know that we will meet again. When I write "you", then it's all of you I am thinking of.

I hardly know now what more to write to you, everything seems so tame. It's just like with the visits, after ten minutes have gone by.

I can't write a will, "He did not leave a fortune."

I can't avoid feeling ashamed that I have put you through all of this.

I'm not crying, what would that help? Try now to take it easy. Oh well— one life failed, what is that against all those lives we can look forward to?

Heartfelt greetings to everyone in the family, friends, and acquaintances. I can't write up all of your names here.

Comfort yourself with the fact that I am not, and you are not, the only ones experiencing this. There are many thousands who are sharing this hard fate with us.

For just once I hope that you don't come to visit.

That Søren didn't get to know his father, that's the burden he will have to bear in this incarnation. It would be stupid of you to tell Søren that he should be proud of his father. His father was thoughtless, although he meant well.

Now it will just naturally turn out, that the war ends, when I am gone.

There is really so very much that I should tell you, but maybe it's just as well left unsaid. You'll find out what has to be done. And what I in general think and believe, you know that after all.

I don't die with any belief that I have been an angel in the 25 years that have passed. There were many things, that I would have done different. But I will have an opportunity to do that. As long as you mature enough so that you don't make the same mistakes again.

If only Lissen will find a man again, and get married. Honestly speaking, that is what I would wish for.

And if only Mom's nerves can make it through this trial. I would be proud to know that Mom does not break down. Tears don't hurt. As long as Mom doesn't become a nervous wreck over this.

Yes— this afternoon Dad and Lissen should have been up to see Dr. Best. Too late! But it probably would not have helped anyhow.

Now I don't know what more to write.

I'm sending thousands of thoughts, and kisses to all of you.

Arne

I didn't get to say thanks for everything, when you were here. Thanks for all the bright— there were only bright—

moments, you have given me. Thanks for your understanding, and forbearance. Thanks for my childhood and youth. That time, that I lived, is anyhow the most beautiful in ones life.

Orla Andersen

26 May 1944 (7 October 1915)

Dear Scouts

Yes, now I have to pack it in. God has decided it that way, and I must follow his command, just like you.

In this life the important thing is to set a goal, fight for that goal, and not to know the concept of compromise. I only have one wish left:

"That you will always behave like good, Danish boys."

"Be Prepared"

Your former troop leader

Orla

Benny Randau Mikkelsen

26 May 1944 (23 August 1925)

Technical student Tester tells the following story:

" I was in cell 385 in Vestre Prison together with Benny Mikkelsen, from May 9th, 1944 until the evening before his execution on May 24th. He had been sentenced to death on Monday, May 22nd, so I had the opportunity to hear his last messages. He wrote a letter there, on some gray wrapping paper, because that was all we had. Unfortunately, I had to swallow that letter, as I was expecting a very strict and thorough inspection before being transferred to the prison camp at Horserød on June 13th. I had read that sorrowful and yet proud letter so many times, especially because of the possibility of confiscation, that I can remember it almost word for word.

The letter was short, and to the best of my memory had the following words:"

Vestre Prison, May 23, 1944

Dear everyone!

Yesterday I was sentenced to death by the German court marshal at Dagmar House. Even before the trial began they told me that I could not receive a pardon, and I didn't know what they meant. But I soon found out. Oh, sweet little Mom, you can't imagine how much I hated them at that moment. A strange feeling came to me. Not a feeling of terror, or fear of dying, but a blind hatred and rage against these cruel executioners. I admitted nothing, and have not given any names, and I am glad about that, as it would have just dragged other good Danish men to their death.

A girl turned me in, one I was going with, miss Rasmussen. She had a friend who was engaged to a Schalburg man whose name I can't remember, but I really hope, that when the time comes, you can have all three of them liquidated.

I am doing alright, under the circumstances, in part because I am locked up with a good Danish man of my age, who is trying to comfort me, and help make these last days of mine go as well as he can. The only thing that could save me now is the invasion; if it comes we will all be free within a day.

I have in fact been sentenced to death, but have not been told when I must die.

One thing is certain, that this murderous regime will not get to see a defeated and broken Patriot.

I shall die. I shall die. Oh, little beloved Mom, I shall die, but it will be with pride and Danishness in my heart. I know, that we will win; we shall, must, and can win.

Now I will say goodbye to you for the last time.

Your son

Benny

Benny was led away at 11:35 in the evening before his execution, and got a chance to write two more short letters to his parents and brother.

Copenhagen, Vester Prison, den 24. 5. 44.

Dear sweet and all sacrificing Mom and Dad

I hope so much that you may see the bright times over Denmark, you dear ones. I hope that I can be buried in the cemetery in Aalborg. I had hoped to see different times in this country myself. Life was short, but beautiful, in my dear home, I hope you can get more happiness from Frede, my dear brother. I hope that Dad will see this as it is, it was my own fault. I haven't always been for you what I should have, but I know that you forgive me, dear, I have thought about you since, and longed and believed that I could have talked with you; I know, I have had such great parents and a good and sweet brother, but death will not divide us, dear little Mom, take courage anew for Dad and Frede's sake. Greet all of my comrades, friends, and countrymen, and they know, that I died as a Dane.

This letter is not written neatly, but I know that you can read my scribbling, so that is a small thing in such a time.

I should write more, but will be content to think. I hope you can get me to Aalborg, there where I belong and live. Death is liberation from everything, but life was beautiful, and therefore I hope you will live many more happy years, dear ones. I can't write all that I feel, but you understand me, I know that for sure, I have nothing to be ashamed of.

Goodbye. I am thinking about you in my last hours, dear ones. Dear ones, a final greeting from your son.

Benny

Thursday night, May 24, 1944

Dear Frede and sweet brother

Yes, little Frede, we have had many happy days, we quarreled a bit, but were friends again at once, such is brotherhood. I wanted to accomplish so much, but accomplished so little, but maybe enough, as was my fate, little Frede; I know, and hope, that you will be a big support for Mom, she has to survive these times, dear; when Dad comes home everything will be good again; I know that, that Dad will be and is, a good man. Now it has been a long time since we last saw him, but he is coming back, we know that. You, little Frede, you will be a happy husband together with your own sweet Oda. Time heals all wounds, you know, many have had to give their lives. Frede, you have to be home a lot with Mom and help her in everything, and watch over her, until Dad comes back. Yes, little Frede, you know me, you know, how I am, but I promise you, I died without a murmur. Do you think, that you can arrange it, so that I come to Aalborg? That is my last wish. And then to help our little dear, sweet Mom, she is so good, you know that, she always wanted the best for us. My summer vacation with our aunt will just be a dream, unfortunately, I would have wanted to go to Fyn and have vacation with our dear aunt, she is so sweet and nice, dear Kristine, but I hope she takes a trip to Aalborg after this, now she has married, thank God.

Yes, dear Frede, death will, I am afraid, separate us, but what is life.

My last loving thoughts and memories go to you and our little sweet Mom and Dad.

We have after all a Dad we can be proud of, right little Frede? Thank them for all the good, all of them in Aalborg.

Goodbye dear two

Yours, Benny

Herold Svarre

8 June 1944 (10 September 1909)

Dear Mama and siblings

This will be the last letter you get from me in this world. I hope we see each other in another and better world. Dear Mama, now please don't take this too badly, I have not always been as much for you as I should have; but of course it will cause you sorrow to lose your oldest son in this way, and my offense is after all very little in relation to the punishment I will get. But I will take it like a man, and regret nothing. I am a Danish man and could not say no to what I had to do. Now, dear Mama, I hope that your big girls and Erik will help you, so that you don't suffer in your old age. Please say hello to all of my acquaintances that you meet after this. So now there isn't more to write about in this world, I pray to God to be with you in the time to come, and I know that He will be, He is with me at this time.

The last goodbye, dear Mama and siblings, live-well

Yours always, Herold

Dear Mama

There is time to write a bit more to you, and I will thank you for the good mother, you have been for me and all of us, you have always had to work hard, but you did it happily, when it was for us kids. Now you should have it good in your old age, and I really hope you do. God will help you there, which is my last prayer to Him.

Axel Sørensen

8 June 1944 (18 February 1912)

Well, my own dear Dad

This will be my last letter, my last goodbye to you, dear Dad. Last night, "Wednesday," I received my sentence, and now I sit and wait for death. Yes Dad, I know, how hard this is for all of you dear ones to get this message, but you must be brave and endure. So at last I want to thank you, dear brothers and little sister, for all the love and kindness you have shown me, and finally I will ask you to be real good to our Dad. That is what I would want to do, but now I can't do that any more.

And then I will thank you, Dad, for the loving and good childhood home that you and Mom gave me. And finally I will ask to be buried next to my sweet little Mom, who so faithfully followed me through life, so I will follow Mom in death.

Goodbye, all of my loved ones, goodbye dear Dad.

I am so grateful; I go peacefully to my death.

Aksel

Christian Ulrik Hansen

23 June 1944 (26 may 1921)

A few hours before daybreak, on June 23, Christian wrote his last goodbye to friends out in the still struggling Denmark. The fight was over for him now. He sent his last greetings to a young Danish girl— a good comrade and good friend from his school years.

Vestre Prison, June 23, 1944.

Faith, hope, love, freedom, truth,

Justice, duty, honor, loyalty.

Dear Inge!

In a few hours the crack of rifles will be heard across the quiet morning landscape. When the sound has died away, a chapter will be closed. This is my last letter. I am writing it to you, because you—despite everything—have been the one who has understood me best. I don't have to write to you, that I will die in peace, and in the faith in that, that I have lived by.

Praise be to God. Soon the time for me and mine is over. Then it will be you, Inge, who must take hold— love in all its mildness. In His hand, which is God in dawn and eve, we are all tools.

I have one last prayer to you— you know, why I will die. Will you tell my dear friends— not least of all those at home—why I had to go this way? Make them understand, that for me there was no other way. "I offered my lance for a King, like crowns with eternal wreaths".

Strangely, for me death has never been the cold icicle hand, as it is for so many— for most. I have lived with it so long, in this last day so intensely, that we now understand each other completely. It is no longer an enemy of life. It is simply the completion of life. Life becomes whole in it— we meet life in it. I would not want to be dishonest here in my very last letter, but in fact that is how it is. Death and life give each other meaning and content. They are both the beginning chapters to the new life. We are traveling— from our compartment window we stare in wonder out at the countryside that is gliding by us. Before we know it we are inside the tunnel. We can't see what lies ahead- only guess at it, because it lives within ourselves.

Now I am climbing the mountain for the last time. First I look out over the land of memories that God in His grace has given me in this life. A beautiful country with valleys and fair hills— there is a church, and there a little Danish farmhouse. I see you all, you big ones and you small ones, who have wandered in Denmark's rose garden with me, you who would fight with me in love and faith. Then I turn my gaze to that country that God has decided that I should only look into: the future's peaceful Denmark, that lies there in the shadow of God's wings. The new time in the new Denmark. Then I set out on my very last journey to the country "Where the crown never grays, where birds don't die, where happiness is shining clear, but not brittle."

But you, who shall wander into that country—the new Denmark—bow down at dawn, and pray to Him in heaven, that He will bless the sign of the cross in the flaming blaze of blood.

Kaj Munk is gone—so many others have gone—and now we are eight, who will follow the same way—with the deep words from Nazareth in mind-

Goodbye Inge—goodbye, Willi—send my greetings to all my friends out there.

I give myself to God

Christian

The following is Christian's farewell letter to his home, written on 23 June 1944, at Western Prison in Copenhagen.

Dear everyone

This will be my last letter to you. In three hours I will no longer be. So therefore this will be at one time my last thanks to you, and my final farewell.

Please promise me not to mourn. There is nothing to mourn over. I would have wanted to say goodbye to you first, but that obviously will not be allowed to happen. Therefore I must try here to summarize it all.

First, thanks Mom and Dad, for what you have always been for me. Your sacrifice has been great. I have, in my life, tried to make myself worthy of your sacrifice. You know me, you know what I have fought for and will die for. Let that live within you, and make our home strong during the present storm. Let it bind you together, you dear five.

So then it will be these three: Faith, Hope, and Love— but the greatest of these is Love: Let love grow in you, let it grow with Him, Who came down here alone to bear and atone for our sins. He too has taken up my sins. It is in the faith that He has absolved me of my sins, in the faith that He will take me by the hand, and in my love for Him, that I will die. Therefore it not without meaning that I die. On the contrary, there is a deep and great meaning in this. Life and death are after all not just opposites; they complement and complete each other.

It is therefore, you dear five, that I shall die. When you get this letter I will be long dead, but let me live among you, let me be among you at home. And send, at times, a loving thought to me, there where I am, and pray now and then for me.

Annalise, Hans, and Bent—be always good to Mom and Dad. Make your home Danish and Christian. Raise your children to love Him, who gave His life for us, and to love the country and people that God has given us. I wanted to do so much, but have accomplished so little. You, little Bent, you are just five years old; you can still continue that which I began.

Dad and Mom, give him get an upbringing so he can continue.

My stock shares shall, as I have written, be used to buy books for Bent, and he should get them on his birthday every year—not schoolbooks, but books about what I have lived and died for.

It is a bit sad to be looking back and then forth again. Back on all of the beautiful bright memories I have had with you dear ones at home, and with my friends. And forward to all of the duties that I thought it was my calling to carry out. But the memories will live on in their own quiet way, and others will carry out the tasks. Send my greetings to all of my schoolmates and friends, those in Farsø, Grandpa and Grandma, uncle and aunt Karen Ramsings.

In two hours the sun will rise. Then the shots will ring out across the countryside. The grass will cry dew, but see; the sun will rise up and kiss the dew and the grass. And home in the garden the flowers will open their sweet chalices. The rose will glow. See the sun rise up. All of you at home. Bend your knee in the sunrise. Bend your knee, and pray to Him, Who would give His life so that we could live. See, the sun rises up over the land, God's radiant sun. Do not cry; God lives and gives His blessing. He will soon put His end to this crying and suffering world; soon He will exchange His loving discipline with His mildness.

And it shall be my last wish, when freedom again reigns— take an orphaned German child to you in my place. For that is what God demands of us, that we shall be tools first for his wrath, and then for his mildness.

Give yourself to God

Kristian

Greet Harold—I think he should go home now.

Emil Balslev

22 June 1944, 11 p.m. (19 September 1913)

My own beloved Gudrun

I have now learned, that in four hours we will all be shot. The sentence was handed down on Tuesday, and my application for a pardon has been rejected. It is hard to think about having to leave you alone with the three children, and I beg you to forgive me, as it was my behavior that put you in this situation. During my time in prison I have found a firm belief in God and His wisdom and grace. Even though we today cannot see any meaning in this, or understand it at all, I ask you to keep to the words: "And we know that all things work together for good to them that love God." These words are in Romans, 8.28, and I ask that they be put on my grave. If you have nothing against it, I want to be cremated.

You are free to dispose of my things as you want. The only thing I ask is that Viggo gets my fountain pen, Poul gets my pocket watch, and our little girl gets my Bible. That might not be worth as much as the other things, in an economic sense, but I don't have any girl things in my possession, and the contents of that book anyhow outweigh all material things. If you can, I ask that in the future you wear my ring. After now 6 1/2 years I have taken the ring off.

Beloved friend, believe in God, and in His justice. In the beginning it will be hard for you, but as some small comfort I can tell you, from a loving heart, that I am not afraid of death. I believe that someday we will meet again with God and be together for eternity.

During the last 8 days I have had the good fortune to be together with a Christian man, and he has helped me through these difficult days.

Keep on living, and receive the future from God's hand. Give yourself to God, and teach our children to find Him, and to live with Him. I cannot advise you on how your future will be, in a practical sense, but I know that dad and mom will give you all the support possible. You know, that you are the only one I have loved completely, and I regret the times that I have hurt you, and especially now that my death will cause you such great sorrow. You might, on my behalf, take the difficult path to the parents of the four comrades that I brought into this situation, and ask them to forgive me for what I have brought upon them.

A short life is over, and it's a life that I often felt was a failure. I have often been aware of my mistakes and shortcomings, and saw that my value as a person was poor, but I had hoped that in the future I would have gotten the chance to make up for things that I had done against you and others.

I depart from here without hatred to any person, which is a feeling that I have never had.

Bring my children up to be good Christian people, who can do their part for a new and better world than the one I am now leaving.

Right up to the end I had hoped to be pardoned for the sentence that was handed down by the court martial last Tuesday, but that was not God's will, so I hope and believe that Jesus Christ has forgiven my sins, and will intercede for me, so that, after all, I will be able to go to God in His heaven. My last words to you will be to thank you for everything you have meant for me. Thank you for your help and faith in me during those few years we had together, and thanks for the children.

God bless you and keep you.

Emil

You will be in my thoughts in my last moment

Midnight, 22 June 1944

Beloved Dad and Mom

At 3:30 am I'll be taken away to end my life. Through these few lines I would like to express my great gratitude for everything that you have meant for me, and to ask for forgiveness for all of the sorrow that I have caused you through the years.

I die with a firm belief in the God that you taught me to know, and with a belief that everything happens according to His justice and grace. Don't grieve too much for me; I'm not worth it.

Thanks for all that you have meant for me, and for your love for Gudrun and my three children. Help them all, as well as you can, and teach them all to love God, and to thank Him for all that he sends.

I will leave this life without fear and bitterness, only with sorrow over the fate that I have brought over Gudrun and you.

The war, that in this moment rages across the world, destroying so much in the mind of man, will someday come to an end, and so I hope that a new and better world will grow forth from the ruins of the old one.

Thanks for everything. We will meet with God.

Emil

Børge Johannes Lauritsen

23 June 1944 (22 October 1916)

Beloved Dad and Mom

I shall die in a few hours, I can't understand it at all, but it's good to die knowing Jesus. You'll see me again in heaven, there where we all shall meet. Little beloved Mom, there is so much that I should ask your forgiveness for, I have sinned so much against you— forgive me, little Dad, forgive me for all of the bad things that I said to you, I have not always acted toward you as I should have, but you, my dear parents, and my siblings, I must have your forgiveness so that I can go home to Jesus. Dear Oskar, thanks for all that you have been for me— you were a good brother— seek Jesus, it is good to serve him at all times. Dear sister, thanks for everything, my own dear sister. Dear Martha, thanks for all your kindness while I was with you. Dear Kissa, you dear sister, thanks for everything. Dear Ninna, forgive the many harsh words I had spoken. Thorvald, Axel, Anders, you good brothers-in-law, thanks for all that you have been for me. Little Jørgen, Oluf, Knud, Erik, Karl George, Ole, Poul, Karl, Bent, Poul, my own little favorite, Torben, Thinks always about your uncle, he loved you— be good boys, and set your course towards Jesus. You must forgive everything, all my dear ones. You must know, beloved Dad and Mom, that I had the best home in the world. And my thoughts were there to my last moment. If only I had been more for you, and I would so much have wanted to see you once more, dear Mom and Dad and siblings, but we will meet again at home with Jesus. My last greeting to my whole family, and to all of those that I held dear. Always be good to each other, I have so many times regretted my bad temper, and the trouble I caused. Little Mom, one day I will see you home with Jesus. Little Dad, you were the best dad in the world. My thoughts are with you in my final hour. May God protect all of you. Farewell, beloved little Mom, you, my own little Mom. Farewell, my beloved Dad. Farewell, my beloved siblings.

A thousand kisses, little Mom and Dad.

Your own boy. I belong to God.

Jesus died on the cross for me. Jesus is my Saviour, and I will soon be home with Jesus.

Jørgen Ryder

22 June 1944 (20 September 1923)

Dear Mom!
Dear Eyvind!
Dear Sister!

Now I know that I am to die in four hours, and I am writing to you to say goodbye for a while, because we will meet again in heaven. We all have to die sooner or later, and fate has determined that I shall die now. Dear Mom, Eyvind, and sister, I die with my faith in God, that God is great, and that God will forgive me for my sins in this world. It says in the Bible "Ask, and you shall receive—seek, and you shall find— knock on the door and it will be opened for you."

Dear Mom, you wrote in your letter, that I got today, "God bless you," and I am sure he will do that, and I know that you have prayed for me, as I have for you too in these terrible times, when the war is spreading death and destruction around the entire Earth.

I pray that you keep up your spirits, for think what Jesus endured for our sakes.

There was so much I wanted to make up for when, as I believed, I would come home to you again, but I ask you to forgive me for what I might have done to cause you grief.

Oh, how I have missed you during this time, I am so fond of you, and there is so much I want to tell you and to thank you for during the time I had lived together with you, and, dear Mom, you still have two of us left. Dad and I will meet in heaven, and we will all meet there, when life down here is over, and I have so many good memories of you from my time, but life goes on, so keep your spirits up, because it will work out, and life doesn't stand still.

In my work with FDF I had not always done as I should have, but I hope that I accomplished something, because it was there I found my call to fight and strive for, and it was there that I sang this little verse so many times

Fight for all that you hold dear.

— — — —

And how true it is, what is said there. It has struck me so many times, when I have been together with my comrades, and how many good times we have had together in the camps, at meetings and rallies, where I had been together with all of them, and I ask God to hold his hand over FDF, and all of my comrades.

I am only writing this one letter, so I ask you to give my greetings to all of my comrades and those I know, for I was so fond of that little town of Aars.

Yes, now it will soon be over, but I am not at all afraid to die, and I ask you, for my sake, to keep your spirits up and your courage high. God bless and keep you, and help you through this life, which at times can seem hard and difficult, but despite everything is beautiful, and seek God when you feel alone.

Now I will send you my last loving greetings and thoughts, which have always been with you.

Jørgen

Jens Peter Funk Lind

23 June 1944 (14 May 1921)

Dear, dear Mom!
Dear, dear, Dad!
Dear, dear, Karl!
Dear, dear, Paul!
Dear, dear, Jørn!

I don't know what I should write to you here in my last, irretrievable, moment of life here on Earth. I have 3-4 hours left. There is so much I should have said, but it is almost standing quite still now. But I know that we will meet again, with God in Heaven.

We all have to die, sooner or later, and now it seems that I shall die.

I am not afraid of it, because I know that God will take me, and that we will all meet by his side. My last wish is that all of you will forgive me, just as God surely will. Dad, Paul, Jørn, and Karl, please take real good care of Mom, be real good to her. There was so much that I was going to make good on, but didn't get around to.

Especially for you, Mom, who had worked so hard for me, that I should have it good, and I did have it good, all too good. Dear Mom, you will forgive me, I know that, and then you Dad, and you boys, it is a shame that you must bear this sorrow.

But, dear ones, there are so many others who have lost their children in this war, and you at least have three left, who, with God's help, will be there to support you, and to make you happy.

I don't really understand that I have to die now, so young, but God has a purpose with it, you must know and believe that.

Fight for all that you hold dear,
die, if that's what's needed,
That way life is not so hard,
and death will not be either.

That has struck me so many times. Dear Mom, give Anna a last greeting from me, and thank her for everything she has done for me.

Say hello to the whole family, Ruth and everyone.

Dear, dear little Mom, Dad, Karl, Paul and Jørn, now I don't have much time left here on Earth, but my thoughts are with all of you, and with God.

Dear Mom, Dad, Karl, Paul and Jørn, I'm not at all afraid to die, and I ask that you keep your spirits high, even though life can sometimes be hard, but seek solace with God, and He will help you.

Now I will send my last and dearest greetings and thoughts, which have always been with you.

Jens

Michael Westergaard Jensen

23 June 1944 (25 October 1916)

Lieut. Michael Westergaard Jensen's parents never received his last letter. They received an empty envelope on which was written:

»Der Brief wurde diesem Kuvert entnommen. Nach erfolgter Uberprüfung, erfolgt die Nachreichung des Briefes.

Hauptw. d. Sch. P.

Michael's cellmates had, in a letter to his parents, told about his last days and hours.

After Michael had received his death sentence, and with a smile stepped into his cell again, it was with the words "the death sentence came crashing down today. I will die for my country, that's the best solution for me, and so I'll get to go on vacation to Hadsund anyhow."

Michael's last days were used to encourage his friends. He didn't even think about himself, all of his thoughts were about his home, and the sorrow that his death would cause his parents. The very last night, before Michael went to bed, he climbed up so that he could look out of the window to see, in the distance, how far along a new construction project had come. Then he went to bed and slept. The next morning he was woken up by a loud German voice shouting "Jensen!" Michael was ready, his face lit up with a beaming smile, and he was at once in his clothes. A firm handshake to all his cell partners and with a "*goodbye, and remember to tell my parents, that I died with that strong faith, that my mother taught me as a child,*" he left the cell, as if he was going to his wedding.

Marius Anthon Fiil

28 June 1944 (21 May 1893)

So, beloved Gudrun!

Now I am ready for the Lord's mercy. Because he will help us all, we, who need it, and I will die in the knowledge that you will hold together everything that is yours, and that you will hold and keep it for the coming generation, and then that generation will let it go on to the next generation, that will live on with our name.

God be with you, God preserve you, and may the Lord show his face over you and all of us, peace in the name of the Lord Jesus Christ, amen.

Kisses from all of us
Yours

Marius, Peder and Niels

— — — —

Greetings, and live well, Niels Kjær.
Churchbells, not to the capitol,
There's a castle in Vesterled.
Fight for all that you hold dear.
Denmark in a thousand years.
Our Lord is such a mighty fortress.
Goodnight, greetings,

Marius

The last kiss, the last handshake
Goodbye, all good is wished for you.
We are longing for peace.
Goodbye, everyone.

Dad, Peder and Niels

— — — —

42

Dear Gudrun, Tulle, Bitten, Gerda, Ritha and Otto!

Many small wishes for the future. None, or just a few flowers, and no fancy headstone. Give money instead to the needy and the church.

Always have a flagpole standing south of the inn. Keep the stone clean, the one in the garden, with the verse, take care of it and keep everything in order, and stand together, children, on that spot, that is the dearest thing for me on Earth— the old inn. Greetings to the butcher. Ellen, Marius, and Mie, Herman and Tulle, Martin and Marie, Ejnar and everybody in town, aunt and Aage, and all my friends in Randers, postman Anthon, Bidstrup-Hadsund, and otherwise everybody.

God watch over our home, that I never will see again.

Your Marius

Dear Otto and Ritha!

Yeah, so we won't see each other again here, but I want to thank you for everything that you have been for me and mom. I wish the Lord's blessing on you. Stand together for mom and our home, you must hold on to everything that is Danish, in your home and on your path, and when you get children, teach them who Niels and Peder were, and teach them everything good, and everything will be well with them here in the world.

There was so much here, I wanted to write, but I have to finish this.

But I do know, that you will help your mother as much as you can, but in the summer you must stay at the inn, and run it as usual. Raise the flag high on holidays, and Ritha, take care of everything that is old and noble.

Handshakes to you, and the Lord be with you. Say hello to your mom and dad, and hello and a kiss to both of you, and the Lord be with you both.

Goodnight,

Your father

Marius Fiil, Hvidsten Kro

Then sing—"The Jutlander he is...." Greetings from Peder. Greet them we know.

> *It shall wave when they are born.*
> *It shall wave when they are baptized in the name of the Holy Ghost.*
> *It shall wave when they as youth promise to do good.*
> *It shall wave when they act and believe in a time of happiness.*
> *It shall wave when they fall, and have served their country well.*

Dad

Dear, dear Bitten!

Grow up big, be sweet towards everyone, and be sweet to your mom. Take care of your home, hold onto your memories; a day will come with summer and sunshine. Compose yourself, and be of good Danish courage. Thanks for all the smiles, that you have sent me.

Kisses and handshakes,

Your father, Marius

Go with God, obey His commands, grow tall and proud, and all will go well for you.

Good night

You father

— — — —

A Danish Swan. Kiss— Kiss for Bitten, be strong.

Your father. Goodnight.

Sing Danish songs, be good to the children.

Always cheerful, when you go. Good night, my treasure.

Your father.

— — — —

Dear beloved Gudrun, Bitten, Tulle, Gerda, Ritha, and Otto and Stump!

Now the clock has struck 11, and soon 12, and we will be leaving here, the Lord is calling us home to Himself, and everything will be good at home together with Him, as good, as a person can have it. We are in good spirits, all of us, because we know, that we are going home to eternal rest in the arms of the Lord. And when all of you dear ones at home stand together for our dear home, and work for it, then at some time we will meet again in the house of the Lord, where there is peace and no war, and until that time you must stand together and stay together and work for home and Denmark's sake, so the generation, that will bear our family name forward, can say "our father fell with honor for Denmark and for our King."

Remember, many have fallen before us. Remember the Danish seamen out in the world. The Danes at home before us, and those after us, we've all done, what we could, even if it was just a little, but we are not ashamed, we say like Blicher: "let us always behave, so our children can be proud of us," and we can be an example for our children, dear Gudrun, and continue with the same upbringing, so they will honor your and my memory, and then it will be preserved into the future. There will be sorrowful days for you, my beloved, with struggle and work, but you have to bear it in the name of The Lord, and trust Him, He has helped me in these last days, you can safely put your trust in Him, and He will help all of you, the Lord will help you, the Lord will keep you, the Lord will shine the light of peace on all of you, and the Lord will be with you all of your days, you dear ones at home.

Your father and your husband, Marius

Niels Fiil

29 June 1944 (12 June 1920)

Dear Ritha, beloved sister!

Many thanks for the years that we have had together at home, now you have to help mom as much as you and Otto can do in this difficult time.

Don't cry over me, I will be fine where I'm going, and I'm proud that I'm good enough that it should happen in this way. Stand together now for our home, and make sure that it stays in the family, and that your first son might be called Fiil, that name must never die, remember that.

Dear Ritha and Otto, thanks for everything that you've been for me during this recent time.

A thousand greetings and kisses

Your Niels

— — — —

Dear beloved bitten

Thanks, dear sister, for everything you have been for me. You have always been the little one, but now you have to be big, now you have to help mom as much as you can, use your little sensible head well, and never compromise, stay on the straight path, it will always lead to the goal.

A thousand thanks. Greetings and kisses,

Your brother, Niels

— — — —

Dear little Gulle

Now if only you can grow up, and be allowed to experience a peaceful and happy Denmark, that which we others have fought for. I hope and believe that it will happen for you.

A thousand greetings and kisses, your uncle, Niels

*With money, life, and blood to the last breath
for Denmark's free flag!*

*Now I hope that God in heaven will be with you all, and
hold His hand over you, and help you, just as He has helped
us through this time, and as He has given us a meaning for
life, in the same way He has given us a meaning for death, so
I go confidently on the way that He has shown, as it is the
right one.*

*Now you must greet all of my dear friends and comrades,
who I have lived together with in this life. Greet Marius and
Mie, Herman and Tulle, and the other's wives and children,
and help each other, as much as you can. Those who come
back have sworn to do everything for you, and I believe them
on their word.*

*Now I will finish this, my last greeting to you and mom,
with these words:*

Fight for all that you hold dear,

Die if that's what's needed,

Then life is not that hard,

And death will not be either

*"To die for our country is to live for our honor." Now a
last loving greeting and a thousand kisses, from*

Your Niels

— — — —

Dear Tulle and Gerda

*Yes, now the hour is in for us, and we have seen each
other for the last time, but I've been happy to be together with
you today, and I'm proud of both of you, you have shown
yourselves to be like brave Danish women should be, and I
know that you will accept this with your head held high, and
I'm proud that I can follow my comrades. I know, that God
is with us, and that He has a purpose in this, and I'm
following confidently on the path, that He has shown, because*

I know, that it's the right way. Now you have to hold your head high, I know that you will help to lead Denmark towards brighter times, where men can speak freely, believe, and think, as befitting a Dane, and I know that Mother Denmark will never forget us; some of us must die so that others might live.

Greetings to all my comrades, give them courage and strength—

It will be okay. Remember, when you get home again, to help mom all that you can, hold our old home together, and make sure, that the name Fiil never dies out. Be well, you dear girls, I hope that before long you are again home with mom.

Remember the verses I have given to you, they will help to comfort you, and it has to work out, for freedom, truth and right will again rule in Denmark.

"For the old, who have fallen, there are new ones everywhere,

Who will meet, when ever they are called "

Now— good courage

A thousand greetings and kisses to you two beloved girls, from your brother, Niels

I go peacefully on my way, for God is with me.

Peder Bergenhammer Sørensen

29 June 1944 (3 June 1914)

Beloved Tulle and Gulle

Yes, now I have to go away, you have to greet everyone, and tell stump, when she grows up, that she was dad's girl.

I'll be thinking about both of you to the very last minute. Now I want to thank you for everything that you have been for me. It will be difficult for you. You're the one, who has held everything together.

I'm proud of you.

Goodnight Tulle and Gulle from your father

Peter

PS. I'm sleeping well now. God be with you, we'll meet again.

Albert Carlo Iversen

29 June 1944 (28 September 1895)

Dear Gusta, Ulla, Tove, and Helle!

Yeah, Now Dad is going out on the long journey. I am sending my last loving greetings to all four of you, and I hope you may live long and happily. Think only good of me, I wanted to do the best, and only wished to make it better for you.

Dear Gusta!

Thanks for everything, and thanks for indulging me, and take good care of the children. Let Laus and Viggo help you, and listen to their advice.

Dear Ulla!

You are a big girl now; help Mom with the small ones.

Tove and Helle!

You must just be good and loving, and remember that you will be happy again sometime. I hope that everything will be taken care of for you, and that you will again have it good. Your father's last thoughts are for you and your mom. You must not grieve; you must remember that some must fall in a war.

And now once again: I am thinking in my last hour about you. Greet everyone from me.

Thousands of kisses and loving greetings to Gusta, to Ulla, to Tove, and to Helle from

Your husband and father

PS. The last kiss and greetings to all of you. Keep your spirits up. Live well, all four.

Einar Axel Larsen

27 February 1945 (16 August 1906)

My beloved Sofie and children

I am asking that you and the children not feel too much despair over hearing this. You, beloved Sofie, know how my case was. Yesterday I was sentenced to death, and today I found out that I will be shot this afternoon, 27 February 1945. When you loved ones receive this letter, I will be dead, and all that I own will belong to my little Poul Erik and you, and I hope it will be of use to you. You, beloved Sofie, I thank you for all the good you have done for me, and if I have done anything against you, then I know you will forgive me, and that you and the children will have fond memories of me.

Little Poul Erik shall have my wristwatch, so I hope that you can see to it that he takes good care of it. Say hi to Nulle, and tell her that she should be a good little girl, and Nina, she is a sweet girl, and I know that you, dear Sofie, will get joy from her, and I hope you will give her a gift for her confirmation, so she can have something to remember me by. And then there is little Poul Erik, I believe he will be a good boy, think about me, little friend, I, who always loved you, be good to your beloved mom, who I loved above everything else on earth. Aage, greet him as well one last time from me. I am sitting with your picture in front of me to the end, and I am not afraid to die.

Dear, beloved Sofie, be with God. Greetings to my little Poul Erik, and tell him I died with a clean conscience, live well all of you, and greet everyone I know. So now I will finish with the final and most loving greetings and a thousand kisses to all of you

Your beloved Einar

Farewell everyone. Keep this letter.

Karl Gustav Stricker Brøndsted

27 February 1945 (13 December 1915)

Fragments of a condemned man's diary

Written in the police station in the spring of 1945 by a communist group leader who, together with two of his comrades, waited for their sentence to be carried out.

Now I am sitting alone and writing this after finally, through the intervention of the head guard, having gotten my things.

After I came down I was put in chains and taken to "Dagmar House," where a number of prisoners showed up. After an hour I was taken into a room where there was a dozen prisoners, including my comrades "Svend" and "Jens", guarded by Hippos.

Time went by slowly while the prisoners, one by one, were taken to the court, which had finally been convened. The Hippos, young swaggering kids, entertained us with raw shouts and brutal demands to stand properly at attention. There was no chance to speak together, and I stood up against a wall and found faces in the wallpaper, and just kept thinking that I must not break down. One of the prisoners that came back from the court was allowed to light his pipe. This, and other signs, said more clearly than words: a death sentence. It was past midnight before the turn came to one of us, namely Jens. Then it turned out that Svend and I would not be taken to the court that night. The three of us were taken back to the police station and placed in the same cell. Despite everything, I could not make myself believe the sentence handed down to Jens: Death. He was reluctant to talk, and had little hope for a pardon. Because of the language problems he had not had chance to say a single word in his own defense.

Jens lay down to sleep on the floor with his cape over him, while Svend talked non-stop about death.

At noon Svend was called to "verhandlung," i.e. to be sentenced.

I was glad to be alone with Jens. As a person he was much closer to me than the others in the group, despite his religious point of view. Once we had kept watch together, and discussed religion all night long. We finally agreed on his principle that honesty and love should be at the core of any philosophy of life. And he is not orthodox, or a proponent of the church as such. In connection with the possibility of a pardon, I declared that it was an obvious task of the church to conduct an action that might mitigate the fate of the wartime prisoners. The church, Jens said bitterly, is an institution, and as such was marked by indecision and tepidness. 3:30 p.m., Jens was called in, and learned his fate: In half an hour he should be ready to be taken away, and at 5:30 p.m. he would be executed by a firing squad. He wrote a letter to his family; I helped him to pack, and then we took leave of each other. We embraced each other. I could not say anything, but Jens said: God be with you.

Preben Richard Christensen

27 February 1945 (8 August 1925)

Dear parents

When you read this letter I am no more. I was sentenced to death yesterday, and have now received notice that the sentence will be carried out by firing squad today at 5:30 p.m. But promise me that you will only have good memories of me, and forgive me for all of the grief and worry that I caused you. Dear Dad, promise me, that you will take this with composure. I know quite well that this will be hard for all of you, but stick together even more after this. Dear Mom! This will be hard for you too, but give everyone the consolation that I died in the knowledge that I had fulfilled my duty. Dear Henning! Promise me, that you will continue with your studies, and that you will help Dad and Mom in this difficult time. And Knud! The memory of you has always helped me. I really believe that you will come home and put back together that which I have destroyed in Dad and Mom's hearts. My belongings and money I give to Henning for his hard work. Farewell now, everyone. I die happily in the hope that you too will agree that I have only done my duty to my fatherland. Greetings to grandma, Tove, and everyone I know. Greet my colleagues at work, both on the 3rd and the 1st floor.

Farewell

Your Preben

Paul Boris Alex Madsen

27 February 1945 (23 October 1915)

Dear Pusser, dear Kurt and little Putte

Today I found out that I will be shot at 5:30 p.m., and this letter will be that last one from me, but the worst thing, that is the thought about how you will get by, little Pusser. Everything that I have goes to you and the children.

Dear Pusser! It is not easy to gather one's thoughts in the final hours, but I want to say thanks for the good time we have had together, and I ask that you forgive me; but the belief that it was a good cause we fought for must help a bit.

Say hello to your dad and mom from me, and all of those down on Lolland, greet Poul, yes, you must give my greetings to all of them.

Dear Pusser! Now you must be a big girl, and give my greeting to little Kurt, and ask him to be a good boy. I had so much looked forward to seeing him become something, to help him move forward, but that will not happen. Little Putte is so little, she'll forget me soon enough, but she is a good girl, and I think you will get joy from her.

Dear little Kurt!

I ask you to be a good boy, and to be good to your mother, and when you get big, to help Mom and Putte.

Now I send many loving greetings from your own

Dad

Dear Pusser

I am so thankful for the time we have had together. I might not have always acted as I should have, but I know that you'll forgive me, as I have always loved only you. My life has been short, but I have had the happiness of having a good wife, and two beautiful children, and that good memory I will take with me to the grave.

Dear Pusser

Now you must have my farewell, little girl, will you greet our two children from me?

Goodbye, little Pusser, and the last loving greetings from

Your Paul

LONG LIVE DENMARK!

Carl Borch Sørensen

27 February 1945 (25 July 1925)

Dear everyone

When you read this I will be with my father, having left this earth. My thoughts are with you in this my final hour. I hope you help Mom through this, and that you will be caring and happy for each other, and understand how much you care for each other, and do not cry needless tears, but hold on to those memories you have of me.

Dear Mom, I am in despair over the deep sorrow I have caused you at home, but you must stand together even more after this, and comfort and be good to each other. I am thinking about Erik, who thankfully does not understand this. Be sweet, and send Ruth my final loving thoughts, and say that maybe we will meet in the other world sometime. Comfort her, and tell her that this was God's will, and don't let sorrow darken her youth. Be happy for life, and enjoy it while you have it, for nobody knows the day before the sun goes down, and that is just as well. Greet the family, friends, and acquaintances, and whoever else feels for you.

Dear Bente, now you must be good to Mom, so she can get that happiness from you that she deserves, after all that she has been for us, and I hope Erik will take my place, which I believe he will, and that you will find joy in your little girl, and that fate will be better for you than it has been so far. Keep my postage stamps, and let Erik have them when he is bigger. You can decide what to do with my money, and anything else of value, but Mom gets to choose first. Understand that it is hard for me to write everything that I would like to say, and that is in my heart in this my final hour. Understand that I fought, and fell, for Denmark's honor.

The last loving greetings to you, Dad and Mom, Sister and Erik and the little girl, and all those I love and know.

Long Live Denmark!

Your Carl

———

Dear Ruth

This is my first and last letter to you, who I loved and was so fond of. You know, that I was not much for writing, but I hope that you will be glad for this final greeting, in which I so want to tell you what my heart longed to say, but I find it so very difficult to find the words. Think about the time we have had together, and let that be a precious memory, but do not let sorrow darken your youth, but enjoy life, as long as you have it. When you read this letter I will no longer be alive, so I am sending you your ring so that you will in no way feel bound, but will look forward to the spring— you'll see, life has many pleasures in store for you, who has already had such sorrow. Greet your parents and siblings, and bring our friends this final greeting. I send you a final greeting from Preben, who stands by my side in death, you know Preben, who you said looked like me, he had the same ideals and goals as me.

Long Live Denmark!

The most loving and tender greetings to you, my love Ruth

Carl

Erik Pedersen

10 March 1945 (5 July 1918)

Dear Dad, dear little Mom, and my dear siblings

So, it has happened, that which we all feared, and that which I have expected would come in these recent days. I have, this morning, been sentenced to death in a German court martial, and I am sending this final letter to you, to bring a final greeting to you, and to say thanks for all that you have been for me in the time that I was given to live here on earth.

Yes, dear parents, it is hard to leave this place, and even though I know that I had disappointed you many times in my life, I know that it will be hard for you to lose me. But we will meet again, for there must be something after this. I give you many, many thanks for all that you have done for me. Thanks for the happy childhood and youth that you gave me. And I will, in my final moment, send my thoughts home to all of you.

I can faintly remember my first days here on earth, when we lived in Copenhagen. But more clearly I remember the days from my childhood on Ribe Street, and the years in school. Can you remember when I had to go to the factory with a lunch for Dad? I was so proud when I went out with that little basket. I could have worked harder in school, and I have regretted that. But my childhood years were happy, thanks to you, my beloved parents. I cannot express, on paper, how thankful I am for all that you have been for me. But I know that you understand me, and forgive me for my sins. I have never found a better comrade here on earth than you, dear Dad; but it took me a long time to realize that, and now it's too late. I always wanted to be the smart one, even though I knew full well that I wasn't, and I am thankful to you, my dear Dad, for all that you had done for me in the time we had together. And thanks to you too, my dear little Mom, no one on this earth could have been a more understanding, loving, and caring mom, than I have had. Many times you had cried yourself to sleep when I had misbehaved; but you always understood me, and forgave me. I also remember now the Christmas eves we had together, how wonderful they were, and also the birthdays, when we would have my favorite dish for dinner, and also for these beautiful and happy memories I give you my thanks. In this hour all of these thoughts from the past flood over me, and thanks to you all of my memories of my dear home are only happy and light, and for that reason it is so much harder to say farewell to all of it.

And thanks to you, my little Sister, many times, for all that you have been for me. As children we did not always get along, but what can those quarrels mean compared to the love we felt for each other during these later years. Thanks, little Sister, for all that you have done for me. I hope that you will be happy with your Erik, for you deserve that more than anyone.

And to you, Ole and Poul, your big brother gives his thanks. You have always been a couple of fresh boys, who I have many happy hours to thank for. Remember, boys, when you are grown— well, you are of course already grown, but anyway remember that you have the world's best parents, and it's to them you should turn with your sorrows and worries, they are the only ones who can really help you, and so you must promise me, that you will always do what you can to make Dad and Mom happy, and remember, if you are about to do the wrong thing, that your big brother, in the final hours of his life, believed that you would do everything you could for Dad and Mom.

I unfortunately don't have a photo of all of you, but the image of the five of you is so very clear in my mind. And in my final moment I will se all five of you smile to me, and say farewell!

Yes, dear parents, I have been allowed to live about 27 years, so it has probably not been my fate to live any longer. But all of my years together with you, thanks to the love you two have shown each other and us children, have been happy years for me. I wish for both of you that the three children that you have left will provide a happy and easy old age for you both, for nobody deserves it more than you two. All your lives you have worked hard so that your children could have it good, and we have had it good. All day long, dear dad, you worked at the factory, and in the evening on your accounts, to provide what ever was necessary, and Mom has always made sure the we had clean clothes, a nice home, and that we were well fed, even though you had to be busy with your sewing machine, but no children have had it better, than we had.

And now it is all coming to an end. And we shall not see each other again in this world. So I am sending a final greeting, and thanks, and say to all of you a final farewell, and live well. May God the Almighty hold His great and loving hand over all five of you. Please greet all my friends and acquaintances from me.

Your son and brother

Erik

Henrik Wessel Platou

10 March 1945 (31 January 1918)

Dearest little Mom

Promise me to take this letter as calmly as you possibly can. I have been sentenced to death today, but I have applied for a pardon, so maybe I'll get pardoned.

There is so much I want to write, but it's not that easy. If this should be my final greeting, then I will ask of all of you to accept my deepest thanks for all the good that you have shown me, and you must not be too sorry about this. I ask you to give my most loving greetings and thoughts to all of my friends and family, and to Gerda and my son. — I am calm, for I know that God is with me. Once again, thanks, and farewell— or maybe see you later, little Mom, you have always been my understanding friend. Greet Dad a lot, when you see each other again.

The most loving thoughts to all of you, and to you yourself

From your Henrik

Hans Silas Nielsen

10 March 1945 (19 September 1918)

Dearest Dad and Mom

It is my hope that you will take the news of my death as calmly as you can. I am, after all, just one of the very many who have had to give their lives in this war. Perhaps I will be spared for a great deal. I am unfortunately not what I should have been, and at an age where others have families, I have not gone very far.

I have saved a little bit, and what there is I ask that you use on yourself, now that you only have your pension to live on, you will probably need it. I had dreamt about being able to help you, but now this will have to be enough. Not many have had a home like mine, and I cannot find the words to express my thanks for all the goodness I have enjoyed with you. My last thoughts are of you, and I would wish that I really could believe that we will meet again. Greet all of my friends when you see them.

And finally I wish for you that you may live peacefully and well for many years yet, and that you may stay healthy so that you do not feel your old age to be a burden.

Your son Hans

Jens Thue Jensen

10 march 1945 (25 June 1922)

Dear Dad, dear Mom, and dear all sisters.

When you get this letter, I will probably be no more. But don't grieve over me; I have died with a good conscience.

My life was short, but I have nothing to complain about.

I have perhaps not gotten as much out of life as I should have. I probably haven't been as good as I should have been, but I meant well. Whatever I did, I did with the best intentions.

I wanted to do the best for everyone, but have probably, at times, acted rather clumsily.

There is a lot in my life that I would like to do over, but I have faith in God, that He will help me, also now through this final hour.

I know that both of you, Dad and Mom, have shown me the right path in life. Especially now, at the end, I have understood that, and I regret deeply that I have not always followed that path. But I have prayed, and still pray, that God will forgive me, and I really do believe that He will hear me.

Do not mourn over me. I believe that I did what my conscience told me, and that, after all, is what we must do in this life.

And I believe that I can calmly meet my fate, as I know that God is with me.

Just think about all those that have had to die like me during this war. That should make it all easier for you, and I know that God will help you through this as well.

Dad, I would like it if, for whatever money is left from my insurance, you could set up a scholarship at the school in Ribe. I think that is the best way the money could be used.

I am sorry that I won't be able to see any of my sisters

again, and that I can't say goodbye to you. But I hope that you will forgive your brother for that sorrow and hurt that he might have caused. To you I will say, that you should continue to follow the path that Dad and Mom have shown you, and everything will be fine.

And now I will just ask that you say hello to all my friends and acquaintances.

With love to Dad, Mom, all my sisters and relatives, and also to Anne Margrete and Aase, from

Jens Thue

(That was the last letter we received from our brother, Thue, after he was executed, just 22 years old, in Ryvangen, 10 March, 1945)

Helge Brock Iversen

10 March 1945 (20 June 1924)

Dear Dad, Mom, and Mogens

Now the hour has struck, my fate is sealed: we will never see each other again. This morning I was condemned to death, and in the time left until the execution takes place I will write to you, my loved ones at home. First I want to thank you for everything that you have been for me.

Now I look back over my short life— now I see everything with different eyes than I had earlier. My childhood had been so happy and carefree. I know that you had always tried to do everything that you could for Mogens and me. You have worked so hard so that we could have it as good as possible, and for that that I am so thankful. I have rich memories from my childhood, richer than any other's.

You, my dear parents, had given us a home that, perhaps, I had not earlier shown my gratitude for. But now, in this last letter, I want you to know that I am so deeply grateful for it.

I am thinking now about our beautiful garden. I had always loved that garden, just like Dad. How many beautiful and happy hours it had given me, that place where, as a child, I most liked to play in. Now I can say that it was the setting for my entire childhood. One impression remains so alive for me today: it was in the winter, I was 7 or 8 years old, it was 7 or 8 o'clock in the evening, Mogens and I were out in the street, playing on our little sleigh, Dad was at the office, working, and Mom was at a meeting. Mogens and I were having a great time, and we sled all the way from Storegade by the railway down to the viaduct— it was so beautiful, and it remains one of my life's brightest moments. I have often thought about that moment, and even now, in the final hour of my life. And then there was school in Bramminge, and that too was a lovely time, and to come home to lunch to see what Mom had on the stove; it was always good food. Yes, I have only good memories from that time— how good you were to me, dear Dad and Mom. But you had great sorrows; Mogens' serious and long illness caused so many worries. But God, the Almighty, helped you through it, and Mogens got better.

Now I will tell you, Mogens, who has a long life ahead of you, do only what your conscience tells you, you will experience many disappointments and trials, but they can be overcome. Just talk to Dad about it, talk with him, he will understand you, and you have friends, as I have had, you can talk with them, just don't keep things to yourself, things that are a burden, talk with someone about it, and it will be all right.

School in Ribe was a wonderful time, it was there I made my best friends, and it was there I got to know so many really good people. In particular my years in high school were good, several of my teachers meant a lot to me, and for that reason, as my last wish, I am asking that you establish an endowment in my name. It shall be on 6,000 kroner; you'll get the money from my life insurance. The interest on that money shall be paid out each year to the best comrade in 3G, and the principal together with the students in 3G shall distribute the money, and it shall not be based on grades, but only on comradeship. I ask as well that you think about the high school club "Hejmdal," give them my final greeting, and give them something that they will be happy for. Give my last greetings as well to the school's teachers, and also to the principal. Yes, they were happy years down there in Ribe, graduation, yes, a great time, which I recall with joy. There were friends who will now be active members of society.

But you, my loved ones at home, Dad, Mom, and Mogens, you will remain, and the little family will be smaller. I give thanks for all of the letters that you had sent me, they have given me joy, and they have shown me that you too have found your way to the Almighty, with Him we have found peace of mind, with Him we will find comfort, He always helps us, and wants only the best for us, and it is with peace in my heart, and the belief that He will help, that I now go into the eternal sleep. I am convinced that He will help you, my loved ones at home, you must not grieve over me, for it cannot be any different, just lift your eyes to heaven, and all will be well.

Now I will finish with this, my final letter to you, and I thank you for everything that you have been for me, thank you for my childhood and youth, for coming to visit me in the prison in Kolding. I send a greeting to all of my friends and acquaintances back home. And finally I give myself into the Lord's hands with the prayer that he will watch over you, my loved ones, and comfort you in your sorrow.

The most loving greetings, and my final farewell

Your Helge

Leif Dines Pedersen

13 March 1945 (3 December 1921)

Dear Dad and Mom

Well, this letter will be my last greeting to you. I received my sentence today. It was a death sentence. I think you have already found out what I have done. I have participated in sabotage in several instances, and implicit in the murder of a German officer, and now it is all over. The thought does not bother me very much, as I have, during the time I have been involved in these things, been prepared that this could happen.

I am only sorry that I have not been able to prepare you. Those times I have been home on vacation, I wanted to tell you, to prepare you, but each time I thought that maybe it would all work out, and then there was no reason for you to know anything. About my motives for what I have done, I can only say that I have done what my conviction demanded of me, and, whether it was right or wrong, the future will show.

It is not easy for me to collect my thoughts, they just fly around, there was so much that I wanted to say to you, but I have trouble finding the words.

Do not think if me as a deceased, think of the good times we have had together, and forgive me for the misfortune I have brought upon you.

On the following pages I have noted a few things, a few greetings, I ask you to give, and some information about my personal matters, including about the student loan that I unfortunately leave behind me.

First of all I ask you to greet aunt Elsa and aunt Margrethe, and thank them for what they had done for me during my childhood and youth. And then there are these two addresses in Silkeborg. One is for my lodgings at Thorsgade 46 (the landlord is grocer Jensen), the other is for sausage maker Skou, Ørnsvej 93. I often ate there, he will be able to help to obtain and forward my belongings.

And at last I send my most loving greetings, and a final thanks for what you have done for me in my childhood and youth.

Forgive.

Leif

The Savings and Loan Company in Frederiksborg forgave Leif's student loan. They wrote the following letter.

"Because your son, during his daring work for Denmark's emancipation, was arrested, and executed in march of this year by the Germans, the leadership of the Savings and Loan Company, in honor of his memory, has decided to forgive the balance on the loan."

Aage Søndergaard

13 March 1945 (9 October 1922)

Dear Dad and Mom

Don't be too frightened over this letter. But you know, when you receive it, that I am probably no longer among the living. Today we were interrogated, and we were sentenced to death. I know that it is a hard blow to you, and why we were given that sentence, we don't understand.

It could just as well have been some others, but now God has chosen us, and we will die as men. I don't know what else I can write, but one thing I know is that I will die with faith in God, and I am not at all afraid. It will probably be an easy death. It will be worse for you. Especially you little Mom, I think so much about you. Also you, Dad, but you're a man, so it will probably not be as hard on you.

This life doesn't mean so much. After this there is an eternity with God, and there is no evil there. But for your sake I will keep up hope to the end. I haven't been as good a son as I wish that I had been, and unfortunately I won't have a chance to make up for the pain that I have caused you in this life. But I die with faith in God. All is transient here on earth, both the good and the evil, but in the next life, which lasts forever, all is good, and there we will all, sometime, join together with God.

The verse that God gave to me at my confirmation:

> *Trust in God*
> *Even when it looks a mess!*
> *Even if the whole world's falling*
> *We can climb all the mountains*
> *As long as our Lord's the skipper*
> *And we honestly endure*

is one that I have enjoyed throughout my life, and I ask that you think more about this, and also about the last verse of "Always joyful." These, and many more, I have sung for myself, both in the free life, and here in prison.

The practical aspects of my death will be taken care of; I mean my belongings in Silkeborg. If they don't release my body, don't worry about it. The flesh will follow its course here on earth. The most important thing, the soul, no one can take from God, it is His forever.

It is a strange feeling to be sitting here and writing to you, when I am actually dead; but because God is with me, I am neither afraid nor sorry for myself. All of my worries are for you and Inge. She will get a letter as well. It will probably be worst for her.

I ask you to greet all of my friends and relatives. Tell them that I will die with faith in God, and I am not afraid. I am glad that I could die for my country. There will probably be many others who will follow after me; but Denmark will endure. It is Denmark we have fought for, and it is for Denmark we have died.

I give thanks to all of you, for what you have meant for me in my life. That it now comes to an end is the will of God, and that is probably the best.

All of my sorrows are for you at home: Dad, Mom, Ellen, and Gunnar, and last but not least Inge. What she has meant for me you cannot understand. You taught me about God. But she taught me to believe in and have faith in Him, and you can believe how much that has meant for me, not least of all during these days. One understands how much life means after being here. You should thank God for every day, and every meal, you get. But as has been said, after this life there is another that is better. I have not always believed that, but now nobody can shake my faith in it.

My greatest wish is that you may all live a long and happy life. You should of course get as much as you can out of this life. For why else was it given to us?

Now I better finish. I will again say to you, that I die with faith in God, and that I am so sorry for the sorrow that I am to blame for. It is all my fault, and I ask that you forgive me. I know that God will forgive my sins, for I believe completely in Him.

So now I will finish with the most loving greetings to all of you: Dad, Mom, Ellen, Gunnar, Grandma, Holger, and Herdis. Yes, I could go on; but you will do that for me.

Most loving greetings

Your own Aage

Paul Mackeprang Nielsen

13 March 1945 (31 December 1922)

Dear Asbjørn

Yes, now the final hour has arrived for me, and I must die. I have given my life for that which I hold dear, namely my fatherland Denmark, and my parents. I believed that with my modest effort I have helped to make Denmark a free and independent country again. I have done my best— I have, after all, given my young life, and my parents have given one of their children, part of the best that they had. I die with an easy conscience. Luther has said: "To go against your conscience is neither right or safe." I have lived by those words, and therefore I must die. I had not expected such a severe sentence as a death sentence, but it must be God's will. I have made peace with myself, and I know that God will be with me in this difficult time.

And you, my dear, best friend, I send you my final greeting. Thanks for your true and wonderful friendship.

My final prayer is for you, that you may help to comfort my parents, and that you will pray for me, so that God will receive my soul. I ask that you greet all of my comrades in FDF in Esbjerg, and everyone else I know. Greet my parents many times from me, and give them my thanks for all of the wonderful hours at home in Esbjerg.

And last of all I ask that you continue your work in FDF for Denmark's youth. Teach them to love Denmark, and all that is true and good.

The most loving greetings!

Your friend Paul

Thanks for everything good

Dear beloved Dad and Mom and siblings

Well, the final hour has come for me. Today I learned that my sentence is a death sentence, and there is nothing to do about it. But I die with a peaceful conscience, because I must, and have, given my life for that which has meant the most for me; your and my fatherland, Denmark. I have given the best that I have, my young life, and you have given something of the best you have, which is one of your children. When you get this letter I will no longer be among the living, but do not be sorry about that, because God is my Saviour, and He is with me at this difficult time, and He holds His hand over me, and gives me the strength and power to get through this with my head held high.

I ask now that you not be inconsolable for my sake, but to seek comfort in God, and I pray that He will be with you until you too, sometime, shall close your eyes for the last time on this earth. Please do not grieve. We will meet again sometime. It's not really that bad. But that is because I believe in God, and had given my heart to Him many years ago. I am thankful for the years I have lived, the beautiful days at home with you, and the wonderful time at FDF, together with Christian comrades. I give thanks for all that you have given me— life, and the days of childhood at home. Vacations, when I was at home. Thanks for that, dear Dad and Mom.

And to my dear brother and sister, brother-in-law, and sister-in-law, I give thanks for all of the wonderful days we have had together. Thanks for every wonderful hour. Thanks for every encouraging word, and thanks for the financial help while I was studying. I ask that you comfort Dad and Mom as well as you can, and help them in this difficult time that is soon upon them. Pray to God for help, that is the best you can do. Help them, so their old age is not too hard.

Why have I fought? Because I believed that in that way Denmark could become a free and independent country, and that was my vision. I wanted to be a part of helping Denmark, and the Danish people. For these thoughts and ideals I have fought, and therefore I now must die. But my

God is with me, so I have nothing more to write. I ask you one last time not to be distraught. I die for a good cause. I send the last loving greetings to you, Dad and Mom, Carl, Axel, Kirsten, Lise, Ingrid, Meta, and Eli and the little children. Pray that God be with me.

The most loving greetings I give to all of you, friends, and acquaintances.

Your devoted Paul

Bent Jensen

13 March 1945 (8 March 1923)

Dear Mom and Dad

At 9:30 this morning I was sentenced to death, and now I am waiting for it to be carried out, which can happen at any time. It is incomprehensible that I will die in a few hours, but I have to say, that I am not afraid. You must not lose courage, remember, that even a sparrow cannot fall to earth unless it is the will of God.

The most loving greetings

From your Bent

Paul Petersen Holm

13 March 1945 (25 march 1920)

Dear two!

Yes, dear Mom and Dad, when you get this letter I will have been taken from the evil that exists in this world. Now take this calmly, it's not all that bad. We will, after all, meet again sometime— we all know that.

Well, I don't have a lot to write, but I'll try to fill up this page. I hope you will have many nice sunny trips on the motorboat.

Yes, Mom and Dad, the hour has come when I must take stock. I know one thing, that when this happens, I will have a clear conscience. I have fought honestly for that which I believed in, for my fatherland and God, as you well know from my last visit. Greet all of those at home, and give them my best wishes for a better future for all of you.

And finally I want to thank you, Mom and Dad, for the wonderful time when we had been together. It was such a wonderful time, until the war came. Give my greetings to all my siblings.

Well, I will finish with the wish that you keep your heads high, and do not be disheartened by this. Stay your course, and our fatherland will go on to be Danish, even if it is little. God will protect you as always, and will help those in sorrow. Yes, farewell, Mom and Dad, we'll meet again. I know that a better time is ahead.

Now the best greetings to both of you from your son

Paul

Svend Egon Nielsen

13 March 1945 (12 June 1924)

Dear Dad, Mom, Carl Arne and Knud Erik

It is difficult for me to write this, my last letter to you, because I know that it will cause such great sorrow, but that can and must be overcome. I have been sentenced to death today. It is a hard sentence, but I am in good spirits, and not afraid of what is to come. I hope that you will take this in the same way, as that would make me very happy, now that all of my thoughts are about you at home. This has been my own doing, and I don't regret anything, and I don't blame anyone for it. I am only sorry for your sake, you have done everything you could for me, and never received any thanks for it. My last and biggest wish is that you, dear Dad and Mom, will take this message with courage, and not be too distressed. I know that it will be a hard blow for you, but you will get through it, and time heals all wounds, and this one as well. Finally I send all of you, dear Dad, Mom, Knud Erik and Carl Arne, the most loving greetings and wishes for a long and happy life in a free Denmark.

Svend Egon

P.S. Say hello to my friends and acquaintances.

Georg Vilhelm Jørgen Stougaard

17 March 1945 (26 October 1912)

My own dear Putte and 3 small girls

Well, dear Putte, as fate would anyway have it, that I should get a last kiss from you, none of us would have believed it, that it was the last time we would see each other, and I am so sorry that I didn't get to see my little girls one last time.

We have just been in to be sentenced, and it was a death sentence, but I have been allowed to write to you. Dear little Putte, forgive me for all the misfortune I have brought on you, and try, I know you can, to give our children the best possible upbringing, and teach them to think about Dad now and then, for I did it all for the sake of our fatherland.

Dear Putte, if you can, get married again, both for your sake and the children's sake, but promise me that they never forget me. Greet your dad and mom, and say to them that I ask them to take care of you in the first difficult time, and that it is forgotten from my side. Dear little Putte, despite how difficult it may be for me to write to you, we are all calm and collected, and we believe in Denmark's future. Dear Putte, I am so glad that I was able to see you, think only of me when I was good to you. I know that I had not always behaved as I should have. Tell Lis girl that Dad has had her picture with him in bed every night, and that she must never forget Dad. She must be a big girl, and help Mom with the two smaller ones. Bente will also be able to remember Dad, and my little sunbeam, if only she could remember Dad.

Dear Putte, greet all of our friends, Lars and Johanne, Dad, and all of them, and think of me with your best thoughts. It may well be that mother-in-law is right, that we will all meet in the end where there is peace and happiness. Dear little Putte, take this in your own loving way, take care of the children, and it will all go well for you. I put all of my wishes and faith in for you, that you will do the best for yourself and for our children. Once more a final and warm kiss to my beloved Putte mom, Lis girl, Bente girl, and

Dad's little sunbeam from your own Dad— a final farewell, and my final thoughts are with you.

Greetings to all of you from uncle Kaj and Kaj Ohlsen.

If only you can get through the first difficult time, my own dear little Putte—1000 kisses— .

Dear little Putte, a little poem I have written for you:

> *May the bronze bell's tone*
> *Sound out very soon*
> *And bring us the message, so all will be glad*
> *That peace has now marched into this land*
> *And gathered together, in Denmark of old,*
> *For the future's burdens, both women and men,*
> *In hope and in faith for our fatherland*

Dear Putte mom, let my little girls read this when they grow up.

My own dear Putte, be a big girl now, never forget me. 1000 kisses, and a final farewell

Georg

Hans Brahe Salling

17 March 1945 (17 April 1917)

Dear Mom and Dad

This letter will be the last you hear from me, I have been sentenced to death today, together with several comrades. You must not be allowed to be sorry about this, I have again found the faith from my childhood, and I am convinced that we will meet again under better conditions. I have, during this recent period, always held the words "Fight for all that you hold dear," before me. Now I will just say thank you for all that you have given me, and I pray that you will forgive me for the times when I had not behaved as I should have. Greet my sisters, and ask them to always remember, that we will meet again, and let them live accordingly, that is my experience, that I write in my final moments. I cannot comfort you any better, and no comfort is necessary, I know quite simply that we will meet again. So once again, live well, and thanks for everything.

And I ask that you greet all of the good people that I have been in touch with, and thank them too for everything, there must be some meaning in all of this, I know that. I am quite calm, and I am fine, for I have, despite everything, peace in my heart.

And finally, my most loving greetings to you, and my siblings, and to all of the people who have helped me on my way.

Live well everyone

Hans

Jørn Andersen

17 March 1945 (9 August 1909)

Dear Else

I have just been given my sentence, and it was a death sentence, so we'll never see each other again. Now you must take this sensibly, and as calmly as you can, my own friend. I will do my best to behave like a man to the end, and I expect that you too will take this with dignity, and that you will greet all of my friends, and in particular Kirsten, and thank them for the times we have had together.

And now I will say thanks to you for the time we have been together. And if you do, and I definitely hope you do, get married and have a boy, then give him my name, and tell him, when he grows up, so that he can understand that I died for that which I believed in.

Well, there is no more to write about, but I expect of you, my own little young one, that you will have the rest of your life to live up to that which we believe in. I hope with all my heart, that despite all of the sorrows you have had so far, and also those you may have in the future, that you will have a happy and good life with a good and wise man—.

The purely practical things I won't bother to write about, as I have no doubt that you will manage them in the right way— Kiss, and the final greeting, my own friend, from your brother.

Jørn

Svend Georg Borup Jensen

17 March 1945 (19 December 1909)

Dear parents, siblings, and friends, and Mira and Palle

Yeah, so this is the last letter you'll get from me. All but one of us has been sentenced to death. — Yes, I have done what all Danish men have, or would have, done. — I have always love all of you, and I hope that you will be good to my two dear ones, Mira and Palle.

I am a bit strange right now, and am taking it well, with an open mind. Now I'll go up to Mother, and I guess we'll meet in time. My final words are: "Fight for all that you hold dear, die if that's what's needed, for then life is not so hard, and death will not be either." Farewell now, the final one, my beloveds. Thanks for all the good.

A thousand kisses and greetings

Svend

Kaj Ohlsen

17 March 1945 (11 May 1911)

Little Beloved

Now promise me that you will not break down completely.

I have just received my sentence, and will be shot in one of the next few days. You must comfort yourself with the fact that I have only followed my convictions, and done my duty.

You must take care of Mom, she is probably the one who will suffer the most, comfort her as best you can. I hope that you get married again and try to be happy. I haven't always been that good to you, but my final thoughts are about you, and I have always loved you.

The final kiss, and loving greetings

Kaj

Dear little Mom

Here is a final greeting from your big boy. You must comfort yourself in the knowledge that he died like a man for the fatherland, and that he did his duty, as you wished that he would do.

You must take some care of Es. She should sell the house, and try to get by as well as possible. It is my wish that she should marry again.

You must greet Carl and Lauritz from me, and tell them that they should be better sons for you than I have been, and to help you with everything that I neglected.

The final kiss, and the final greeting from your boy

Kaj

Kaj Leo Kristensen

17 March 1945 (7 November 1917)

Dear Parents

This is a final greeting from your son Kaj, as today I was sentenced to death. Now you must take this bravely, Mom and Dad and Sigvald, because you must remember that I fought for what had become holy for me. And I will die like a man. Remember, Mom, that I have always said: "Die, if that's what is needed." I am calm and collected, if that is of any comfort to you. I have a special wish for you Mom, and it is for the sake of my other siblings: take this with your head held high, so that you can go on to live for those left behind. I know that it will be hardest for you to read this letter, and to go on living. But you must, Mom, for that is the last thing I ask of you. Now greet all of them, Sigvald, Ragnhild, Elly, Albert, Henry, and Edvard, and tell them that I am taking this like a man. So farewell, little Mom and Dad. My final thoughts are with you. The most loving greetings to you, and thanks for all that you have been for me.

Your Kaj

Mom, just remember, we shall all be going from here, sooner or later. I know, that this will be a hard blow to you, but you two shall get through it.

Live well, Dad and Mom

Ejnar Ole Mosolff

17 March 1945 (26 April 1925)

Dear Dad, Mother, and Mille

I am writing my final letter to you, to thank you for all the goodness that you have shown me. Today I have been sentenced to death for my acts, but I am not afraid to die, as I believe that I have used my life for the sake of Denmark. Greet everyone in the family, and thank all of them for what they have been for me. My final wish for you is that you do not grieve for me. If you can promise that, then I will be happy.

Father, Mom, and Mille, God will hold His hand over you, and grant you a good and happy future. I believe we will meet each other after death, and in that faith I go to my death with peace in my heart. God be with all of you.

Loving greetings from

Ole

Forgive me, that I have not always been as I should have. As a final greeting I am sending my ring to you, Mille.

God be with you

Ole

Bent Christensen

29 March 1945 (6 February 1927)

Dear Dad, Mom, Birthe, Alice, and Grandma

I hope that you take this sensibly— I have been sentenced to death today. I realize, that it will be a hard blow for you, but I am taking this in stride, for I know that when I am dead it will be the end of it. But you must take this sensibly, and just be proud that I die for my country's honor, the best death one could want.

I thank you, Dad and Mom; none could have been better parents than you.

Greet everyone I know.

These will be my last words, I cannot write any more, as I cannot gather my thoughts with death hanging over my head.

A final farewell from

Your Bent

Bendt Stentoft

29 March 1945 (17 May 1925)

Dear Mom, Erlan, Jørgen, Ellen, Asta and little Nanna, Ole and Niels

Today a court marshal sentenced me to death. I am not afraid, but I am sorry for you, little Mom, you have suffered enough already, especially when we lost Dad, but be brave, for we will all meet again sometime. Forgive me, Mom, that I had not told you anything about this, but I was young, and rash, so you'll probably forgive me. And so I can meet death, knowing that you care about me, and that I have done nothing wrong. You must not lose courage, but be brave for your own sake, and for the sake of your children and grandchildren. I have permission to write more letters, but I will suffice with this one, as I know that you will greet all of the family from me, and all of them I know, and give them a picture of me, if they want one. Put a greeting from me on Dad's grave. I hope also that he would have forgiven me. Please fulfill my last wish that you do not lose courage or be sorry about this. The most loving greetings to all of you— especially to you, my own little Mom. Greet everyone, yours forever.

Bendt

Just remember, that I am not suffering, and I have only done this for our beloved Denmark.

Henning Børge Hansen

28 March 1945 (29 January 1925)

Dear everyone at home

The very worst has happened. I have been sentenced to death today by a German court marshal. But you must take this calmly and sensibly, as it was God's will that I should go this way so early, so it must be the right thing.

I will thank you for all that you have been for me— especially you, little Mom, no one could wish for a better Mom here on earth. It is painful to have to say goodbye, but I will die for Denmark's sake, and so it's not that bad.

I am giving my things to little Olga and the little one, always be good to her. For this must be just as hard for her as it is for you, you can believe that. You must comfort her all that you can, promise me that.

I ask you to greet everyone I know, including my father in Odense.— I can't think of more to write, so I will close my last letter to you with a thousand thoughts, and with thanks for everything good.

Farewell

God help you

Henning

Lennart Greve Ahlefeldt-Laurvig-Lehn

28 March 1945 (4 May 1916)

Dear Uncle Andreas and Aunt Ibeth

I must, unfortunately, tell you that today I have been brought before a court marshal, and sentenced to death, and that my application for a pardon was immediately denied.

For my own sake it is of no consequence, I will lose my life for my fatherland, and that is the happiest thing that can befall any man, but especially for Father and Mother, and all of you who are fond of me, it is a terrible thing. I blame myself at times, out of respect for Father and Mother, that I ever got involved in this. But on the other hand, one's parents are not as much as one's fatherland, so when it comes down to it, I believe that I acted properly. So I ask that all of you, for my sake, be happy, because I will die for Denmark's cause, and do not despair. And I ask Aunt Ibeth and Uncle Andreas to help Father and Mother through this.

Thanks for all the goodness, dear Uncle and Aunt, from

Your Lennart

— — —

Dear beloved Parents

Now you must be brave. The worst has happened, I have been before a court marshal today, and have been sentenced to death.

I am not afraid, but for your sake— beloved parents— I am extremely sorry. You will suffer from this loss, but always remember why I died, remember, that I died for my country, the most honorable death one could wish for. So instead of being sorrowful, be happy and proud.

Promise me that, Father and Mother, and then I will be able to die happily.

It is hard to collect one's thoughts with a death sentence hanging over one's head, but I am surprised at how calm I am, but it is just difficult to know where I should begin, and where I should finish.

First I want to thank Father and Mother for everything. None could have wished for better and lovelier parents. Then I will ask that Father and Mother greet all those I know, first and foremost Axel and A.S.,* also Herman, the children, Aunt Ibeth, Uncle Andreas, Aunt Julie, Uncle Peter, Aunt Else, Uncle Tage (I have bequeathed Iver the Reedts Thottske silverware, as I thought it should go back to the family). Greet Gutte, greet Uncle Erik and Uncle Julius, greet the Mouriers, and thank them for the time at Brahetrolleborg, greet Sporon-Fiedlers, and anyone else I know, — cousins, acquaintances, Anine, the forester's Kaj and Thea, give all of my foster children something of mine, so that they can remember me. It is so strange to be writing this letter so calmly and coldly.

Think that I will never see Hvidkilde again, never take a walk home, never see my sister, Herman and the children, or Axel, or you— beloved parents. Oh, if only I could have the vision of your happy faces in front of me—happy, because I gave my life for Denmark. Promise me— oh promise me, parents, that you will be brave and happy. Remember that it will be good for our class, that we had one who gave his life for Dannebrog. That, which is happening now, is the will of God, and God knows what is best.

It really bothers me that I was so dumb to stay at that hotel, instead of moving in with an acquaintance, but then I would have been taken there instead, and would have endangered them as well.

Beloved parents, you can come at any time to get me, so I will finish for now, and write first to Axel, Iver, Aunt Ibeth, and Kaj. I don't know if I can write to my sister— I am not allowed to.

Thanks for everything, my most beloved parents. Remember: hold your heads high.

Your Lennart

What should I write—there are millions of things—In spirit I am standing up on the hill south of Trollekrogen, and look out over the most beautiful place in the world, over Lehnshøj—it is strange that both of us only reached twenty-eight. I tried, for your sake, to be pardoned, but it was refused—it is as if it has not yet sunken in that I shall die—but I am so exhausted—it must of course be nerves. All of my plans are over—there will be no busy farm, no horses, cows, or pigs. No—I cannot continue: Promise me not to break down—but be happy—I die for Denmark.

Thank you, thank you, beloved Father and Mother

*A.S. was his sister, and "the children" were her children. His sister lived in Norway, and for that reason he was not allowed to write to her.

His brother leased Lehnshøj farm. He died in an auto accident in 1937.

Dear Kai

I am writing to you as my cousin, but most of all as the future head of the Ahlefeldt family.

I have been before a court marshal today, and was sentenced to death, and my application for a pardon has been denied.

It is of course a heavy blow, not so much for my sake, but for Father and Mother's sake. Now they will lose their second son. Oh, how will they be able to get through this? If only I knew that they could be happy and proud that their son died for Denmark's cause. — Would you and Thea help them, because the thought that they will be in sorrow, that is what really hurts me?

But I also want to say, that not only am I happy that I will die for Denmark, but also, and first and foremost, that it is an Ahlefeldt that this befalls.

The old motto, "An Ahlefeldt never runs," still applies, and I hope that you, when you become the head of the family, will undertake your duties for the family's advancement and honor.

Greet Thea, and I regret that I must pass as godfather.

Your cousin

Lennart

Eigil Bruno Wendell de Neergaard

29 March 1945 (7 July 1913)

Dear Trold, Mom, and everyone

All of my dear ones, now you must not be too sorry about this, I was in court today, and the judge sentenced me to death, so that will be the end of this. I have been given permission to apply for a pardon, and I am sending that in now. If it is my fate that we shall never see each other again, then I wish you all the best for the future, and take good care of the children, and raise them to be good and clever people. Let them help you, Trold; those who can and will, and don't let false pride spoil your life. Dear Mom and Trold, I have so much to thank you for. Thanks for everything. I think a lot about you in these hours. I have, after all, a slight hope that that my application will be granted . . . Don't let the children forget their father. Tell them about him, and I hope that you will all be happy again, and be well together again . . . I am well and calm, and have it as good as one can have it now. I do not have any more to write . . . to you dear ones I send my most loving greetings and best wishes. Dear Trold, I love you so much, and dear Mom, I am so very fond of you, but now, perhaps, I will soon be meeting Dad.

Now I will finish with the most heartfelt greetings, and a loving kiss for Peter and Vibs from Dad. Dear Trold, I love you. Live well all of you, and farewell, all my loved ones.

The application for a pardon was—as Bruno de Neergaard expected, and prepared his family for—denied the same day, Holy Thursday. At the bottom of the letter, written with a fast but sure hand, in ink, were the following lines:

A final greeting; it is all over. I will die as a Danish man.

Dear Trold and Mom, let me rest in the place alongside Dad.

Love

Your Bruno

A long time friends of Bruno de Neergaard's, who was also in prison, was able to exchange a few words with him on that same day. He was quite calm, even though he new what was going to happen, and he regretted nothing.

"But I would anyhow liked to have seen Denmark free! It is sorrowful, that one shall now be shot."

Aage Emil Daugaard

29 March 1945 (11 May 1911)

Dear Father, Sister, and Peter

I am so very sorry, my dear ones, that I must deliver a terrible message. As you have probably already heard, I was arrested on the 16th of February by the German security police, and today have been sentenced to death. I was given permission to apply for a pardon, so it is now in God's hands what will happen to me. I hope that they will take into consideration the fact that I had taken part in any direct attack on the German army. My greatest wish for you is that you will take what comes with composure. If it should turn out that I must go, then I will ask to have my remains sent home, and that you be given my effects. Dear father, you must not travel over here. I am with you every day in my thoughts, so you must give my heartfelt greetings to all of our family from me. So I will place everything in God's hands, and send you the most loving greetings.

Aage

My final loving greetings! God be with us all. Farewell

Aage

Peter Wessel Fyhn

6 April 1945 (13 June 1920)

Dear Dad, Mom, Ole, and Birte

This is an awful letter that I have to write to you, but I have no choice. I wish so much that I, in some soft and quiet way, could have just whispered in your ear, so that you would not be so frightened, but just a bit surprised over this news, which cannot be otherwise.

Dear good people! When you read this clumsy letter I will already be in another world. And there, just as here, I will have only one wish— that you will help and comfort each other to the best of your abilities, and that you will soon calm down again, and continue with your quiet lives. You should know, that during this recent period, and as always, I have thought of you with an indescribable tenderness and love that I never showed as I could have wished. You should also know that now, when I know with certainty that I shall die, that I am at ease. I have had plenty of time to prepare myself, and I am at peace with this. I just feel this indescribable sorrow because I have not returned your kindness and love when I had the chance, but during the recent years have only given you worries. Forgive me, that I have not behaved as I should have. And now I have to bring you even more grief. If only you can soon get over this, and again be healthy and happy people with your hearts open for all the beauty that life, despite everything, has to offer. Now you know my last wish, that you shall grieve as little as possible over me, preferably so little that other people do not even notice, because it is none of their business. And try to see on the bright moments that, strange as it might seem, there are many of.

I can hardly be happy that I must depart now; it would not be natural at my age, but the way it is going to happen is all right. I have always wanted to know it in advance, so that I could be prepared.

And the reason that you will lose me— it could have been even worse. Not that I am proud of it, and all that nonsense. Now I have no more time. All of this applies as well to Birte, who this letter is also belongs to.

Loving greetings. God be with you all.

Peter

- - -

I feel so distraught now because my unfinished letter got sent off yesterday. The plan was that N.N., who I sent the letter to yesterday, was going to first acquaint you with the situation when it was all over, so that you could have been spared the waiting and not knowing. Now, because you anyhow know about the situation, you might as well get all of the details.

That I have once again seen the light of day is something that none of us four (Jørgen Winther, Greve Ludvig Reventlow, Kim Malthe-Bruun) are able to explain. Yesterday morning, after all four of us had been before a German court marshal, and been given the death sentence, we were driven here to wait for it to be carried out, which should have happened within hours. I was only half finished with the letter to you, and had not yet written to Bit, when we were taken away for the last time. It was just in the last minute that the order was countermanded. We were, mildly speaking, somewhat confused, but anyhow were driven back here. If it should mean a pardon, or just a postponement, we have not been told, but will hopefully know before long.

So now you too are waiting, and not knowing, which I had so much wanted to save you from. It has given us some hope, but I hardly dare believe it, that one could be that lucky. But how I would wish for that, for all of you back home, who have been in my thoughts during this last trip.

My situation is, after all, that I have been a step ahead of you in this, as I have known about the danger for a long time. I have done my utmost to come to terms with this, and I have been happy for having had this chance to settle up while I still have the time. But still one can pray and hope to stay alive, which of course means so much to me, having you four at home. I have completely overcome the pain of having to depart. Now there is just the unbelievable sorrow that you will come to suffer much more than myself. I felt that so strongly last night, when we all four thought that the final hour had come. We were unbelievably calm, and behaved quite normally, even during the trip back. We could smile to each other (those three are truly magnificent boys) and look at the trees with their big buds without bitterness. And I think too that the other three have made peace with themselves, and with God, and feel peace in their souls. It has been so much easier than I could have imagined, and I feel some remorse that it is you who will feel all the pain. When I try now to comfort you, I can only do it by telling you about the thoughts that have helped me through these days.

As I said yesterday, I am quite all right with the way it is going to happen. There are thousands at this time who do not get a chance to come to terms with themselves, and even worse, never get a chance to send their final thoughts to their loved ones.

And the reason that it most likely will end now could be a lot worse. I have no reason to be proud, because what I did, I had to do as a man, and as a Dane, and if I had not acted I would never have been satisfied afterwards. I deeply regret that I had not been more careful, and for that reason have caused you sorrow, and so I ask for your forgiveness, but that I have done my duty I of course cannot regret. You have given us boys a happy childhood, and a good upbringing, to be independent, and now, in this difficult time you continued to send letters and packages, which showed your kindness and love, and have made these months seem like a vacation. I know that it's natural to think about the things that you forgot to say and do, when you are inexorably separated from your loved ones. And that is what I am doing now, but believe me, you have nothing at all to blame yourselves for, and I am not even able to say thanks for all that I owe you.

What I in particular must thank you for is that you never forced any religious dogma onto us. We were allowed to find out on our own how we should feel in that decisive aspect.

100

And that should be the greatest comfort of all for you. During these months I have not only found myself, but also my God, and I will die, no matter whether it's now or in 50 years, with the hope that something exists after this. When that is the case, then 50 years more or less is of little importance.

If I have to take that drive again, which we did a rehearsal of yesterday, then I know, just as the first time, that I will feel the greatest pain from thinking about your feelings when you have to accept the truth of what has happened. Therefore I ask that you do not grieve over me, but try to accept it, not as a tragedy, but as something that is unavoidable, that had to happen sooner or later, as it must for everyone. The price we pay to live is that we all must give our life sooner or later.

For all of you I wish that better times might soon come, so that you can forget all this, and again find peace and harmony in your lives. You still have so many obligations, and you'll always have the duty to help each other to be happy.

If it should be all over, then, when the war is over, I would like to be buried by Pastor Teglbjærg in consecrated ground at Jægersborg church. He is a good pastor and a good man with a positive view of life.

Please be especially good to Birte, who may feel even worse than you will in the beginning. But also try to get her to forget all this, and to start over. I would wish for her that she might find another, and a better one, who could be as good to her as she deserves.

Dear people, I think that we have now seen the brutishness, which may, but hopefully will not, become a reality. I wrote yesterday to N.N., as with his connections and his name, he has the best chances to help. I have also sent an application for a pardon to Dr. Best. We have the right to hope, so long as we at the same time are not afraid to look truth in the eyes, as it may well turn out to be.

But most of all, keep up your good spirits. If I can trust that you will, then I can promise to take that final drive in good spirits, if that should be the case.

All that I can feel and think of good thoughts and wishes is for you.

Peter

Kim Malthe-Bruun

6 April 1945 (8 July 1923)

Dear Mom

Jørgen, Niels, Ludvig, and I were court-martialed today. We were condemned to death. I know that you are a strong woman, and that you will accept this. But listen, it's not enough that you simply accept it, you must also understand it. I am just a little thing, and will soon be forgotten, but the ideal, the life, the inspiration that filled me, will live on. You will find that inspiration everywhere— in the trees in spring, in the people you meet on your path, in a sweet little smile; you will meet that which perhaps had value for me, and you will love it, and you won't forget me. I will still be able to grow up and mature, I will live with you, whose heart I once filled, and you will live on, because you know that I lie ahead, and not, as you might first have thought, behind. You know what had always been my fondest desire, and what I thought I would become. Follow me, my dear Mother, on my way, and don't dwell on the past, but rather on that last bit of life that I have had, and you will perhaps find something of value for her, who is my young one, and for her, who is my Mother.

I have followed a path that I have not regretted. I have never betrayed what was in my heart, and I think now I can see a connection between things. I am not old, I shouldn't die, and yet it seems so natural, so straightforward. It is just the sudden way that frightens us at first. Time is short, and I can't really explain it, but my mind is completely calm. I would have been like Socrates, except there is no audience. I feel the same peace as he did, and I really want you to understand that completely— you, Hanne, and Nitte. You must give my greetings to Nitte, I am so full of love for her, and stand by every word that I wrote to her.

It is very strange to sit here and write this document of life. Every word is permanent, it can never be healed, never be erased, and never forgotten— I have so many thoughts. Jørgen is sitting in front of me, writing a confirmation letter to his daughter. A document of life! We have lived together, and now we will die together— two comrades. I have talked with Poul. We had so many different opinions, but he knows what I believe, and what I can give.

And finally there are the children, they have been so close to me in this recent time, and I had looked forward to see them, and to live a while with them again. My heart has beaten with happiness with the thought of them, and I hope that they will grow up to be men who see more and deeper than just the path. I hope that their spirit thrives freely, and never under biased influence. Greet them from me— my Godson and his brother.

I can see the direction that the country is going in, and I know that Grandpa will be right. But remember— and you must all remember— that the dream must not be to return to that time before the war, but the dream must be, for all of you, young and old, to create not a narrow, but a true humane ideal, one that all shall see and feel as an ideal for everyone. That is the great gift that our land is thirsting for, something that every farmer's son can look forward to, and know in his heart that he has a part in, and will work and fight for.

And finally there is her, who is mine. Make her see that the stars still shine brightly, and that I was just a milepost. Help her along, now she can be very happy.

In haste- your oldest and only son, Kim

My own little young one

Today I was tried before a court marshal and condemned to death.

What a terrible message for a little girl of twenty years. I have been allowed to write this farewell letter, and what should I write? How should my swan song be written? Time is short— thoughts many. What is the last and dearest that I can give to you, what do I possess that I can give you now in parting, so that with sorrow but with a happy smile you can live on, grow, and be great.

We sailed the wild ocean, we met each other like playful children, and we loved each other. And we still do, and we will continue to do so, but one day a storm separated us; I ran aground and sank, you were washed up on a new coast, you will live on in a new world. You must not forget me, I don't ask that, why should you forget something that is so beautiful, but you must not be dependent on it, you must travel on just as lightly, and twice as happy, because life gave you on your way the most beautiful beauty. Tear yourself loose, let this happiest of happiness be everything for you, let it shine as the strongest and clearest thing of all, but only let it be one of the golden memories, don't let it blind you, so you can't see all the beauty you have in store. You must not be sad, you will grow and be rich, do you hear me, my own dear young one?

You will live on, and have other beautiful adventures, but promise me, you owe all that I have lived for, that the thought of me will never stand between you and life. Remember that I am a seed in you, and that if I leave you it only means that the seed lives on. It should be healthy and natural, but not take up too much room. And gradually, as bigger and more important things come along, it should slip into the background and become a part of the soil that is full of happiness and growth.

If you feel a tearing in your mind, that is sorrow they say, but Hanne, look farther, we shall die, and if I pass away sooner or later, neither you nor I can say if that is good or bad.

I am thinking about Socrates; read about him, and you

will hear Plato say what I feel right now. I feel a boundless love for you, but no more now than I have always felt. But nothing is tearing at my heart now, that's the way it is, and you will understand. I have something that is living and burning in me— a love, and inspiration, call it what you will, but something that I have not yet found an expression for. Now I will die, and I don't know if I have lit a little flame in another mind, a flame that will survive me. And yet I feel at ease because I have seen, and I know, that nature is rich, and nobody notices if a few seeds are trampled under foot and die. Why should I despair when I see all the abundance that still lives on?

Lift your head, my heart's dearest seed, lift your head and see; the ocean is still blue, the ocean that I loved, and that had engulfed us both. Now you will live for both of us. I am gone and what is left is not a memory that will make you a woman of style, but one that will make you alive and warm, mature and happy. Nothing about lifting yourself up to sit on top of sorrow, because then you would become stiff and holy in your belief in me and yourself, and you will lose that which I loved most about you, your femininity.

Remember, and I swear to you that this is true, that all pain turns to happiness, though only the fewest will ever admit that to themselves. They wrap themselves in pain, and the habit makes them believe that it continues to hurt, and they stay wrapped up in it. The truth is that after pain comes depth, and after depth comes life.

Look Hanne, someday you will meet someone, one who will be your love, and the thought of me will shoot through you, and maybe you will have a faint feeling that you betray me, or something that is pure and holy in you. Hanne, look up again, look into my smiling blue eyes, and you will understand, that the only way you can betray me would be by not following every natural instinct. You see him, and let your heart meet his. Not to drown your sorrow, but because you love him with an honest heart. You will be so very happy, because you will have found a ground where even for you unknown feelings will grow fertile.

You must tell Nitte, I have thought so much about writing

to her, but don't really know if I have time. It is as if I feel I can do more for you. You are the essence of all life for me. I must breathe all the life I have in me over into you, so it can continue to live, and as little as possible go to waste, as that is just my nature.

Yours not forever

Kim

Jørgen Frederik Winther

6 April 1945 (26 April 1917)

Dear Ester

Today I was before a court marshal, and was sentenced to death. That the punishment should be so hard cannot be helped. The most idiotic of it all is that it is not a punishment for me, but for you and our little girl. I am in no way afraid to die, but it pains me to think about the sorrow that you will feel.

The whole world is now full of war widows for whom this message, that you are now receiving, has also been a terrible sorrow. But they have gotten over it, and you too must get over this. Millions have suffered my fate in the fight for the cause they believe in, and I cannot say that I regret anything, for I do not believe that I could have done anything else.

My death means that one more "Hero" has fallen for his country, and my name will be written in history's forgotten pages. But for Susanne, my death will cause a deep-rooted hatred of those who deliberately killed her father. You must stop that hated—it is of no use. During the time I have been imprisoned I have been fine, and have been treated well. That I have to fall now, just a few days before the end of this war, is though a bitter fate.

Jørgen

Ps. I will try to write a little letter that you can surprise Susanne with at her confirmation, but not before.

Poul Erik Krogshøj Hansen

12 April 1945 (6 October 1924)

> *Fight for all that you hold dear,*
> *die, if that's what's needed,*
> *That way life is not so hard,*
> *and death will not be either.*

Dear little Mom

Yes! So it has happened this way. I was taken on Friday, 23 March, right after I was released from the hospital where I had an operation for appendicitis. After being interrogated, we were taken to West Prison, and today we were sentenced to death. I don't know when we'll be shot, but it will probably be today. My own dear Mom— You know I have always loved you so much, and I am most sorry for your sake, for you who are left behind. But you should know that we will go to our death with our heads held high, and maybe we'll see each other again another place.

Live your life for Palle now, and I hope you will have many happy hours together. You know, that a sparrow does not fall to the earth if it is not the will of God, and I believe that He has a purpose for all of us.

Greet Palle many times, I will write a letter to both Dad and Else. God bless my own Mom, and give her the strength to get through this. Never forget me.

The most loving greetings from your own son

Poul Erik

Thanks, Mom, for everything that you have been for me.

Greet pastor Dalsager

A final greeting, and live well

Dear Dad

This will be the final greeting from your son.

I have been before a court marshal today, and sentenced to death. It is a hard blow for you who are left behind, but think about us, and remember, that we are taking this calmly. I hope that you and Mom will sometime be together again at home with Palle, and experience many happy hours together. Think about me now and then, and be good to Mom and Palle, as they need that now. I have also written a letter to Mom and Else. Live well now, all of you, and greet Palle, and tell him that he has been a good brother, who has proven to be a real man, and that he will be a good son for you and Mom, now that he must take the place of two. Dear Palle, always be good to Mom and Dad, and be a brave young man.

Dad, I know you are a good man, take care of Mom and Palle, and greet all my friends and relatives from me.

God bless all of you.

Your son Poul Erik

A final greeting, and live well

Henning Wieland

12 April 1945 (26 December 1922)

Dear Dad, Mom, and Kirsten

It is with great sorrow that I have to inform you that I will never see you again. I have, together with four comrades, been sentenced to death. I am sure that you, as good Danes, will get through this sorrow, and especially you Mom, must be strong. I will think about you to the end, and thank you for being the best parents one could have, and for all the good you have shown me. I hope all the best for you in the future, and I hope Kirsten will be a good Danish woman. I am in good spirits.

Greet all of my friends from me. And here is a final greeting.

> *Fight for all that you hold dear,*
> *die, if that's what's needed,*
> *That way life is not so hard,*
> *and death will not be either*

A final farewell

Henning

God save all of you

Knud Petersen

12 April 1945 (8 October 1925)

Dear Dad, Mom, and all my siblings

Today I was sentenced to death by a German court marshal. I still don't know when the sentence will be carried out, but it probably won't be long. I am not afraid to die, and I am calm. And when I die, I am just glad that I can die for Denmark, my beloved fatherland. Now you must not take this too hard, but be proud that you have a son who can die for his fatherland.

Flemming can have my watch when he is confirmed. I left 100 Kroner at Grandpa's. You can use them to buy something for each of the children so they can remember me. And send a ring or something to Lise. My brown trousers are at the big tailor shop near Vesterbro Place, under the name Ole Schou, Gl. Kongevej 7, and I left my cotton coat with Dr. Krabbe.

So now I will finish with the most loving greetings to all of you, and say thanks you to Dad and Mom for all the good you have done for me.

Many loving greetings. Live well.

Knud

Dear Grandma

Well, we've seen each other for the last time. I was sentenced to death this morning by a German court marshal. Please don't take this too badly. I am calm, and not afraid to die, because I know that I die for a cause that is worth it. Greet Dad many times, if you hear from him. Dear Grandma, thanks for all that you have been for me, for all of your kindness, and your love for me, but do not lose courage because I am no longer here. For you still have Helge and the others, be just as kind and loving for them as you have been for me.

So I'll finish now, and wish you everything good, and once again thanks.

Loving greetings, live well

Knud

Dear Lise

Well, we have seen each other for the last time. I will just send this final greeting, and thanks for everything you have been for me. Today I was sentenced to death by a German court marshal. Greet your parents many times from me, and give them my thanks for the great hospitality that they have shown me. Greet all of our comrades from me. And finally, thanks for everything.

Loving greetings. Live well.

Your Knud

Jørgen Erik Larsen

12 April 1945 (22 December 1923)

Dear Mom, Dad, Knud, and Kirsten

I send here my final greeting before I die. I have for just an hour ago been before a court marshal, and have been sentenced to death together with Otto, Henning, and several other of my comrades. Well, that's the way it went, although I had not expected that, but I am calm and proud to the end, and my last thoughts are about you, and all the good you have done for me over time. I know that this will be a hard blow for you, but I hope when you know that I die for a cause I believe in, that you will understand and appreciate that, and that it might relieve your sorrow. I know that it will be a hard blow for Kiss, and that she cannot take so much. So my last wish is that you will comfort her in her sorrow. Kiss is the only one I have ever loved, and she is the sweetest and best girl I have ever known.

But now I will finish this, my final letter, with best wishes for everyone, and greetings to all.

My final wish is that you will be able to take this in the same way that I do.

Jørgen

My final wish is that Kiss should have whatever she wants of my personal belongings, first and foremost my watch and my ring.

Jørgen

Live well. Think about Kiss. Greet everyone.

Iver Peder Lassen

19 April 1945 (11 July 1923)

Iver's parents, Niels and Fredericia Lassen, received a
farewell letter that was apparently written in a car on the way
to the place of execution. The letter was found when his body
was disinterred on July 2. In Iver's pocket they found the two
letters from home, and a little stub of a pencil. On one of the
envelopes the following message was written:

> *Dear Dad, and my good little Mom*
>
> *Now I am off on my final journey, but I am not afraid,
> for I am going home to my heavenly Father. I have confessed
> my sins for God and for man— forgive me for that which
> God has forgiven.*
>
> *We will see each other in heaven.*
>
> *Your son, Iver*

Ferdinand Emil Martin Andersen

19 April 1945 (13 January 1918)

Dear beloved Helle

Just a few words so that you'll know where I am. You may send some tobacco, all you can get hold of, and some fine cut as well, so that I can roll my own cigarettes; also clean clothes, but no biscuits or anything else. Things are going well, under the circumstances, and I hope that it continues to go well. How are the children? I'm sure they are enjoying the good summer weather. I miss them a lot, just as I miss you, little Mom. How is Grandma? I guess you are over there now and then.

It is a good thing that you have Dad and Mom, and good friends to help you. I am glad for that, greet them from me. Take good care of the children, little Mom, for they are all that we have. Greet them many times from Dad. Do they still say their evening prayers? I think of them every night at that time. If it doesn't go so well, we have at least had some good years together, but we'll hope it all goes well. And now I will finish, with many loving greetings, and kisses to my four best.

Kiss the little ones from Dad.

Ferdinand

Dear Dad and Mom

Thanks for your greetings, and all the good you have done for my four loved ones. It's good that they have you. Keep your spirits up. Hopefully all will go well, but otherwise see to it that the children get a good upbringing. And finally, best greetings from your thankful Ferdinand.

Greet Edith and Levi, and give Vena an extra treat.

Karl Gustaf Kolding

19 April 1945 (21 January 1917)

Dear Rosa

If you received this letter, but haven't seen anything of me within 14 days after the end of this terrible war, then I have set out on the long final journey.

"Little Mom," I had hoped that this would not turn out to have such an unhappy outcome for us, and so close to the end of the war. You mustn't think that I have experienced physical pain in captivity, but spiritually it has been painful from the very first day; I have thought a lot about the meaning of life, and what happens when you die. I have prayed to God for strength and courage, and that He will stand by my side, and forgive my sins, and let me come home to Him.

While we were being driven over here I met a young man from Fredericia in the car, Helge Hermann. You probably know him from the Red Cross. He knew you; he was a department chief in FDF. I asked him if he was a Christian, and he said yes, so we talked quite a bit together. I asked him to help me so that I could find peace in my soul, and so that I could believe, and he helped me really a lot. So now I hope that I will be able to find the path on my own, as we unfortunately could not be in a cell together, but he promised to pray for me, so that I might find peace through him. And I asked him to pray for you as well, that you too might find God. I believe that when you just have the right faith, then everything is good. You should have seen how calm he was, and when I asked him about that he said that he could only thank God, that he wanted to live longer, but that if he had to die, he was prepared. You see, that is how I want to be, and I pray everyday that it will be that way.

Little Mom, I ask that you seek God, and that you seek His protection, and follow Him for your and Birthe's fate. Then you will see that it is not such a burden to be without me, and you will know that I have gone with peace in my soul, and faith that God will take me under His wing.

I am not happy about dying, I would so much want to go home to you again, and be able to be your provider for some years again, but if I shall die it must be God's meaning that it shall be so, and you must promise me not to blame Him, but rather to seek Him, and to pray for strength to go on living, and to raise Birthe in the right way, in His spirit, and with faith in Him, and let us thank Him for the years we have known each other— we have had after all six happy years, and just think that there are so many who were not able to have each other so long.

Please greet the whole family, both in Aarhus and in Fredericia. And let my Mom and Dad see this letter, so hopefully they will find some comfort in learning that I had finally opened my eyes for that which has value in this life, as it is so sorrowful that we must often go so long before we open our eyes, and we believe that as long as things are going well we can get by, and then one day we realize that that is a big lie, and I just hope that it is not too late that I have realized this, but Hermann said that it is never too late, and I place my trust in that being true, and that God will hear my prayer, and let me be one of His children. Yes, Little Mom, you can see that I have begun to take stock of myself, and it is just as well to look fate in the eyes at once, I still hope it won't be the death penalty, but I have begun to prepare myself for the worst, and I have prayed to God for strength and courage, and I do believe that He has given it to me.

Yes, dear Rosa, it is hard to say farewell, there is so much one would want to say, but thank God we were able to talk things through the last Sunday we were together, and you know so much of what I feel inside, and you know how I was, so I hope that you can imagine all of that which I have not been able to put into words, for you know that it would take a whole book. Little Mom, you will of course bring Birthe up in the Christian faith, and with faith in her land and people, and teach her to be a good Danish girl, tell her that her Dad had to die because he was Danish, but do not let her think I was a hero, because I am not even close to that, on the contrary, I am and always have been a coward, but let her understand that there was a time when it cost something to be a Dane, and that her father was one of those who had to pay with his life so that Denmark could be free. Little Mom, I cannot in any way say that I regret what I have done, as it was in no way a crime, and I have gone away for a good cause, and I hope it might be an advantage for me when judgment day comes, and I must be held accountable, and it may well be necessary by then that I have as many good points as possible.

Now greet everyone I know, and wish them all the best for the future, and promise me, that you will be a good friend for Birthe, watch over her, and keep the evils of the world away from her as long as possible, and think about me every time you look at her, she is the fruit of our love, I would so much have wanted to be able to raise her, and to have given her a little brother or two, but it isn't going to be that way. Kiss her many times from me, and teach her to love her mother and be good to her, now that she has no father to take care of her mother.

With respect to the finances, I am not too worried, as I believe that those left behind will be taken care of.

Now I had better finish, for I cannot write an entire book to you, even though I would like to.

Little Mom, I love you, and ask you once again to be of good courage, and not to worry about me, I am sure to find God, so look forward to the day that we will see each other again.

Once more many thanks for what you have been for me, pray for me, and pray also for those people who have taken me, and for those who have executed me, they will surely need many to pray for them.

And finally, the most loving greetings and kisses to you both

Farewell, and live well

Yours forever

Gustav

Eluf Preben Månsson

19 April 1945 (4 August 1919)

Mrs. Månsson, who helped her husband in the illegal work, said that there was no farewell letter from her husband. In his last letter, she says, her husband made no mention of having been sentenced to death. She wrote:

"That he might have expected it could, however, be seen from the last lines, where he explicitly asks me to greet his mother, and to think about her happy smile. The last war was the direct cause of my father's death. My husband knew that if anybody could help me through the time to come, it would be my mother.

But my husband did, however, manage to write a few comforting words. On the back of a small photo of me, he wrote— that he was at peace with God, and had peace in his heart, he asked me to greet his parents, my mother, and our siblings, and to thank them for what they had been for him. And finally he asked me to read psalm 116.

I would actually prefer that the following words be printed in the memorial, because I know that, even though I am writing them, they are also an expression of my husband's thoughts while he was engaged in the fight. My husband and I did not feel any pride in being involved in the fight— but we felt happy and thankful that we were able to take part, because we too could be used in the fight for Denmark's freedom."

Henry Jacobsen

19 April 1945 (23 August 1918)

Henry Jacobsen's wife received this letter on the same day that he was sentenced to death—the last letter from her husband.

Dear Grethe

I hope you are all well. I am fine, and I'll be getting out as soon as I have served my sentence, however long that is, I don't know. We were transferred to Western Prison by car on 11 April 1945. The address is: Henry Jacobsen, born August 25 1918, Western Prison, German Police Section, cell 156, Copenhagen. I can receive packages and letters every 14 days, just like in Kolding. How is it going with little sister, Karl Aage, and you, Grethe mom? I miss all three of you. Greet my parents-in-law many times. I would like to have a picture of you and little sister. If you can get one of her I would be very happy for it. Please write to my parents, and ask them to apply for permission to visit me here. I think I can have a visit from one person each month. Have you been able to do any thing with the garden, and gotten peat and firewood home?

Now, the most loving greetings to you, Grethe! Send some writing paper and envelopes.

Your Henry

Erik Gerhard Andersen

21 February 1945 (24 February 1916)

Dear Dad, dear everyone

This is the last letter from me. I have just been told what is going to happen. I am completely calm and clear, and I regret nothing. I hope that you take this calmly, and do not break down. Life neither begins nor ends with me.

I will not write to each one of you. I will make this as short as possible. I ask that you thank everyone who has meant something for me— and you can say that I am going into this with my head held high.

Loving greetings to all from

Your Erik

Knud Møller

13 February 1945 (25 November 1929)

Knud Møller managed to smuggle out a farewell letter from Western Prison, written on toilet paper. It was the only letter that he was able to write.

To his siblings he wrote:

To put it bluntly, you should not expect to see me again. I am going to be interrogated today, and will be subjected to "other methods," because I refuse to admit that I am a spy, a freedom fighter, or a publisher. Furthermore, they want me to inform on my comrades and accomplices. — — Now I hope that all of you have a good summer, and a happy future. Greet — — and all those I know and are fond of.

To his mother he wrote:

— — If only you will promise me, Mom, to enjoy the summer fully, and rejoice over nature and freedom. There is no way around this. We have to endure what we are faced with, before we can achieve liberation. The worst sorrow will eventually become a sad memory. — — We get yard time every morning, but we are not allowed to talk to each other. Outside of the fence there are beautiful tulips, and later there'll be roses. I hope we can soon have visitors. — — If I get out of here again, I'll start from the beginning, and we two will live together, and it will be great. I guess anyhow that what matters most in life is that we can be something for each other.

Those from the Shell Building

The Shell Building in Copenhagen was built in 1932 as headquarters for Shell Oil in Denmark. It was taken over by the Gestapo during the German occupation of Denmark in WWII, and was used as their headquarters. The Germans knew that the building could be a target for aerial bombardment, and tried to prevent that by using the upper floors as a detention center for Danish freedom fighters. It was known that the Gestapo had archives and material about the resistance that could be used to identify its members. The Danish resistance sent a request to the Allies to bomb the Shell Building, in the hopes that some of the prisoners could be freed, and that vital information on the resistance movement could be destroyed. That request was granted, and operation Carthage was carried out on 21 March 1945. The building sustained heavy damage, but there was a great deal of "collateral damage" as well.

Eleven Danish patriots from the Shell detention center were executed on 9 August 1944. They were not allowed to write farewell letters, but excerpts of letters written to family members are given here.

Jens Martin was a member of the 1944 Group. Aksel Jensen, Gunnar Dahl, Victor Mehl, Carl Preben Berg Sørensen, and Knud Gyldholm were members of BOPA, and Preben Hagelin, Erik Nyemann, Kai Schiøth, Edvard Sommer, and Per Sonne were members of Chr. Ulrik Hansen's group, Holger Dansk.

Victor Bering Mehl

9 August 1944 (6 February 1911)

This is an excerpt from his last letter to his mother:

During these past months I have lost none of my contempt for the Germans. They do not understand at all that freedom means the same thing for a small country as it does for a large one. They can put on a mask, and erect fences, they can tempt us with promises and money, but their cruel system permeates everything that they do, and as long as I can draw a breath I will fight against them.

May a mild rain fall over the fields of our friends, so that the harvest can be golden!

The most loving greeting from a son

Your Jens

— — —

A premonition prompted Victor Bering Mehl to write the following words on the back of a photo of his wife and son

To the memory of him, who for ten years was yours.

Greetings

Your Victor

Sweet in life and sweet in death

And sweet in memory

Aksel Jensen

9 August 1944 (13 February 1919)

This letter was written on toilet paper, and smuggled out 22 July, 1944

Western Prison, Green Section, 14 July 1944

Dear little Mom

Thanks for your lovely letter. It shows that we are of the same blood, you and me, and that you completely understand that fascism is the enemy, and that an honest worker must fight against it, wherever it might appear—even if that should cost the most valuable thing he has—life, and thereby happiness for his loved ones, and you know that I have never compromised my ideals. And I have not done that this time either; I could not passively stand by while others, who have my sympathy, fought a battle that was mine, without me being a part of it. I did not achieve all that I wanted—and now I am here, waiting, and during this time it is good to see that you, Mom, accept it in this way. I am proud of that, I am proud to be your son, and I will calmly take whatever comes my way.

Everything here just moves along at the same pace, only interrupted by the interrogations (12 to 16 hours without bread or water). I must, out of consideration for myself—and those I hold dear—and out of consideration of others here—and outside—weigh my words carefully as on a jeweler's scale—and still answer at once, if I am to avoid a thrashing with a rubber truncheon (during interrogation I have handcuffs on, so I am an easy prey for a beating). For the sake of appearances I let them beat a few obvious lies out of me, as that looks better all around. Otherwise everything is pretty sad out here. Thank God that one has patience, and during the day can let go of all the worries—but in the evening, when I am in bed (without Birthe's goodnight), the telegraphers begin to exchange the day's events; the new ones fumbling and unsure, the older ones automatic and monotone like machine guns, and then all is hushed and quiet, and we hear only the footsteps of the guards in the hallways, and the small talk of the patrols outside the walls—that is the worst, and then the thoughts fall mercilessly upon one, and they all carry the same smoldering embers: Will you see Mom again? Will you and Birthe be happy again? Will it be death? Was it worth the sacrifice? —— Oh, it is terrible!

If the worst should happen, then don't think about our misfortune, but think that 30 Soviet girls have their beloved, 10 English wives their husband, and 30 American children their father, instead of you having me—but we hope that I can make it, and that we will all see each other again before too long. Happy birthday, greet everyone, and may freedom live.

Loving greetings from

Aksel

Knud Erik Gyldholm

9 August 1944 (9 July 1914)

Dear Anny

*It was sure nice to hear from you. I got your letter on 31
July. I am happy that you are in good health, and in good
spirits, as also I am. You've probably started work again
after your vacation. It was for sure some beautiful weather
you had. You can believe that I was jealous, but whatever,
we'll get our revenge another time.*

*Dear girl, it made me happy that you used your vacation
to get out a bit rather than just sitting at home with your
head hanging, as you'll just get sick from that, and it leads
nowhere. No, chin up, and be happy, you'll see that it all
works out to the best. I am happy that my good bicycle has
been taken out again; there is someone who has taken the
chance and thought, that he wouldn't need that anymore. You
can believe that I am happy for the picture of the living room,
with you on the balcony, but my dear girl, you must not go
and use money on me. You have enough to deal with already.
If I can just get some clean clothes now and then, and
something to smoke, then I am satisfied. And don't buy
books either; you can borrow some from friends and
acquaintances. But I am happy that you show that you think
about me, but buy something for yourself, and then I'll be
twice as happy.*

*And finally, many, many loving greetings and kisses from
yours, and only yours*

Knud

Erik Nyemann

9 August 1944 (6 April 1922)

Dear Mom

Now you must not go and grieve too much over me. I am sitting here, thinking back on my life, how warm and strange it has been. Christian (Ulrik Hansen) gave this description of me: an ill-mannered bloody country boy, who bends over carefully and sniffs a lily. If I get free again, I will really do some painting! Even life! At one time I didn't even know what I wanted to paint. Now I know! I am optimistic enough to think that we will all be able to celebrate Christmas together again this year. I think a lot about the future, when I will only have to think about art. Greet Litten, my friends, and Bizzie Høyer, who never finished my painting. I wish all of you sun and happiness, especially little Finn, who I so much look forward to seeing again.

Loving greetings

Erik

(This letter was received in Skive on the day that Erik was executed)

Dear little Mom

You probably think that it is just lies and drivel, when I say that my spirits are at their very highest! A person who has never acted contrary to his conscience should never despair. A thousand loving greetings to you and everyone

Your Erik

Per Sonne

9 August 1944 (10 April 1921)

Dear everyone

Thanks for your visit. Dad, that was sure nice of you to leave home for a couple of days just to see me for barely ten minutes. Thanks as well for the books and tobacco. It is really a pleasure to swap out the bread crusts for a good cigar. Despite all the good advice and warnings, I can't deny that I got a real headache the first couple of days, but it sure tasted great—despite the headache. The only thing that bothers me when I smoke is that my tongue is a lot more sensitive now than it was before I changed my residence, but with persistent training I think I will eventually achieve rather good results in the noble art of smoking a pipe. It sure was a nice package I received on the 27th of July, but you should not be sending me your entire ration of tobacco. And while I am on about the package, please give Mogensen many thanks from me for going to the bother of bringing the package out here, and then waiting around for my dirty clothing. In the next package I would like, beside the usual stuff, a tube of toothpaste and a piece of soap, and finally some matches. I can't buy matches here, and it's a shame to have tobacco but no light. My spirits are high, and after getting my books I have enough to do, so the time goes fast. My health is relatively good, and now I am getting "Sunshine" in the form of D vitamin, so I am not suffering. I would rather have the effects of sunshine in a more direct way, but that will come with time. I am soon finished with nervous system physiology, and will start on nutritional physiology later in the week, but it is a thick and difficult book, so I will have plenty to do for a while. You have probably noticed the date of the letter, it is tonight that the duck hunting begins, can you remember, last time we met after the first day of hunting, Dad, that is now three to four years ago.

The most loving greetings to all, and with hopes that we will soon see each other again.

Per

Kaj Holger Schiøth

9 August 1944 (12 March 1921)

Dear Mom

It was so nice seeing you out here, though you looked a bit tired, but that is not so strange. Little Mom, you should not worry about me at all, I am fine, as you saw yourself, and in good spirits, even when I do not have visitors. My only worry is about how you are doing. I have not yet gotten your letter, but I'm sure it will soon come. Have you bought peat; otherwise I think you should do it? You must promise me not to be in low spirits, you should be happy, and be well.

You are still my faithful Thursday's friend. You have no idea of the excitement one feels before the package arrives, and the relief when it finally does. I am happy over each day that goes by, for then it is one day less until I see you again, though I hope I won't see you out here anymore. Every day I thank my friend Fate, that it has been such a good friend that we will see each other again. On Thursday: soap, one roll of toilet paper, shorts, spinach, "From the Piazza del Popolo," "The Seven Pillars of Wisdom," and if you can manage it, chocolate. And then I won't demand more, except for the discharge, but that will probably happen one of these days.

The most loving greetings and thoughts to all of you

Kai

Eduard Frederik Sommer

9 August 1944 (12 December 1922)

Dear Family

Today we were given permission to write home, and that suddenly gave our brains an unusual piece of work— to form thoughts into words, black on white. The time runs when you let yourself get carried away from here with your thoughts and dreams. A little humming is also allowed, and I have been through the entire repertoire 100 times. Otherwise I am fine, with my own room and entrance, and board, etc. The food is good, and they treat me well. I get fresh air every day. My spirits are high, and they will remain high to the end. I am glad for the Ludo game, and have become a champ. Otherwise I read the Bible that I got last Friday. These twenty lines cannot contain all of them you should greet, but you know whom they are that I value outside of the home. I think about all of you every day, and come to regret something now and then. I hope I can again get to write something, but otherwise, live well, and don't think too much about this here. So! Live well! My heart still beats for Denmark. Commit yourself to God.

Lasse

****

APPENDIX

Hvidsten Gruppen

The group of resistance fighters known as "Hvidsten Gruppen" (The Whitestone Group) is very well known in Denmark. Their story was told in a book of the same name, written by Axel Holm, and Published in 1945. It was also the subject of a Danish film produced in 2012.

Members of Hvidsten Gruppen

1. Marius Fiil
2. Niels Fiil
3. Peder Bergenhammer Sørensen
4. Johan Kjær Hansen
5. Niels Nielsen Kjær
6. Henning Andersen
7. Albert Carlo Iversen
8. Søren Peter Kristensen, (no letter)

Kim Malthe-Bruun

A biography of Kim Malthe-Bruun was published by his mother, Vibeke Malthe-Bruun in 1945.

Kim was executed together with his friends, listed below.

Peter Wessel Fyhn
Jørgen Frederik Winther
Ludvig Reventlow

Jens Thue Jensen

A biography of Jens Thue Jensen was first written and published by his sister in 1992. The title is, "Thue og hans tid," (Thue and his times) and describes the development of the resistance in the area around Esbjerg and Ribe in southern Jutland.

He was executed together with his friends, listed below.

Hans Silas Nielsen
Helge Brock Iversen
Robert Nielsen Pedersen

The following Danes were also executed, but did not have farewell letters in the published book. There are, however, photos and short bios for each of them.

Jørgen Eivind Schacht
Carl Jørgen Larsen
Helmer Andreas Fabricius Wøldike
Poul Ib Gjessing
Hans Jørgen Henriksen
Søren Peter Kristensen
Svend Glendau
Harald Christensen
Preben Gylche
Ib Fischer
Hagbard Friis Jensen
John Erik Andersen
Helge Ove Jensen
Erik Koch Michelsen
Poul Larsen
Preben Lytken Madsen
Ole Bay Andersen
Asger Linderup Mørup
Erik Briand Clausen
Ludvig Greve Alfred Otto Reventlow
Hans Eeg
Helge Herman
Ole Christensen

Hans Christensen Just Petersen
Jens Jacob Wolf Martins
Carl Helmuth Preben Berg Sørensen
Gunnar Mogens Dahl
Preben Hagelin

The following eight Danes were also listed in the alphabetical register, but no photos or letters are in the book.

Carl Erich Abel
Henning Møller Andersen
Herman Boye
Erik Crone
Johan Kjær Hansen
Niels Nielsen Kjær
Andreas Bronislaw Wadesloff Nielsen
Johan Jørgen Tejlmann

<u>Books in English about the German occupation of Denmark</u>

War Games
Denmark on the Eve of the Nazi Invasion, April 1940
Torben Tvorup Christensen
Historical Trust Publishing
Madison, Wisconsin, 2009

Conquered, Not Defeated
Growing up in Denmark during the German Occupation
Peter H. Tveskov
Hellgat Press, 2003

Darkness over Denmark
The Danish Resistance and the Rescue of the Jews
Ellen Levine
Holiday House, 2000

Danish Resistance Members
Books LLC
Memphis, Tennessee, 2010

Danish Unity
A political party between Fascism and Resistance
1936-1947
Henrik Lundbak
Museum Tusculanum Press, 2003

Courage & Defiance
Spies, Saboteurs, and Survivors in WWII Denmark
Deborah Hopkinson, 2016 (has extensive bibliography)

The Boys Who Challenged Hitler
Knud Pedersen & the Churchill Club
Phillip Hoose, 2015

The Danish Resistance
David Lampe, 2016

Refusing to Crumble: The Danish resistance in WWII
Michael Burgan, 2010

Sixth Floor: The Danish Resistance Movement,
And the RAF raid on the Gestapo Headquarters.
Robin Reilly, 2002

Sparks of Resistance
Nathaniel Hong
University Press of Southern Denmark, 1996

Occupied:
Denmark's Adaptation and Resistance to German
Occupation 1940-1945
Nathaniel Hong, 2012
Frihedsmuseets Venners Forlag

Boats in the Night
Knud Dyby & the Rescue of the Danish Jews
Lur Publications, 1999

Mogens Høirup
An Extraordinary Story of an Ordinary Man
Hellgate Press, 2009

Hornet Flight
A story from the Danish Resistance
Ken Follett
Signet, 2003

Books in Danish about the German occupation of Denmark

A complete list of Danish books about the occupation would require many pages. It is a subject that has been written about extensively, and anyone who is interested can search on Google.dk. There are hundreds of books, both historical non-fiction as well as fiction. There are also many films about the occupation.
A very short list of selected books is given here.

Den Politiske Modstand Under Besættelsen
Oluf Pedersen
Gyldendal, 1946

Besættelsens Fem Onde Aar
Redaktor H.Hansen
Kandrup & Wunsch, 1945

Syv Aar I Søgelyset
Svend Carstensen
Hasselbalchs, 1945

Der Brænder Endnu En Kerte
Letters from Prison
Magda & Leo Kari
Fremad, 1965

Der Brænder en Ild
A collection of stories
Printed illegally, without author's names
Folk og Frihed, 1944
(Reprinted in 1945 with author's names)

At Handle med Ondskaben
Collaboration during the Occupation
Hans Kirchhoff
Gyldendals, 2015

www.ingramcontent.com/pod-product-compliance
Lightning Source LLC
LaVergne TN
LVHW011239080426
835509LV00005B/554